Editorial Project Manager
Lorin E. Klistoff, M.A.

Editor-in-Chief
Sharon Coan, M.S. Ed.

Cover Artist
Brenda DiAntonis

Art Coordinator
Kevin Barnes

Art Director
CJae Forshay

Imaging
Ralph Olmedo, Jr.

Product Manager
Phil Garcia

Publishers
Rachelle Cracchiolo, M.S. Ed.
Mary Dupuy Smith, M.S. Ed.

Dr. Fry's Word Sorts
Working with
Onsets and Rimes

Author

Edward Fry, P.h.D.

Teacher Created Materials, Inc.
6421 Industry Way
Westminster, CA 92683
www.teachercreated.com.

ISBN-0-7439-3711-2

©2003 Teacher Created Materials, Inc.

Made in U.S.A.

The classroom teacher may reproduce copies of materials in this book for classroom use only.
The reproduction of any part for an entire school or school system is strictly prohibited. No part
of this publication may be transmitted, stored, or recorded in any form without written
permission from the publisher.

Table of Contents

Introduction

About This Book

Onset and rime lessons are an important part of phonics instruction. *Word Sorts: Working with Onsets and Rimes* is a great way for students to manipulate onsets and rimes in a fun and meaningful way! The exercises encourage students to learn the concept of "onset and rime." The task for the student is simply to sort the words so that they fall into groups that have similar rimes (the vowel plus following consonants).

The book includes the following word sorts: single letter onsets with long and short vowel rimes, blend and single letter onsets with long, short, and other vowel rimes, and triple sorts with less common rimes. The easier sorts are at the beginning and more advanced sorts toward the end. Most of the sorts contrast two rime families. However, in the last section of triple sorts, there are three different rime families.

The word sorts contained in this book are for the very beginning reader. They do not require any reading ability. Students may not know how to read all the words, but they will know most of the word meaning once they have been read aloud. These exercises will encourage the student to pay more careful attention to letter clusters that form rimes.

Note to the Teacher

These word sorts are by no means a complete beginning reading program. However, the word sorts are useful supplemental activities. The activities can be used in a center. The word sorts can be done individually or in a group setting. The activities can also be used as a quick assessment of each student. It is highly recommended that in conjunction with these word sort activities, students hear stories being read aloud to them and have many opportunities to tell their own stories orally.

The teacher may point out how the onset (the beginning consonant or consonant blend) can change the meaning. This is also an important part of phonemic awareness. If the teacher wishes, he or she can take some of the lessons, or even just one of the word families and show how they can be read aloud. This encourages the students to get involved in understanding that words can be sounded out.

Directions: Cut out the words below. Then sort the words so that all the *–ad* words are together and all the *–ag* words are together.

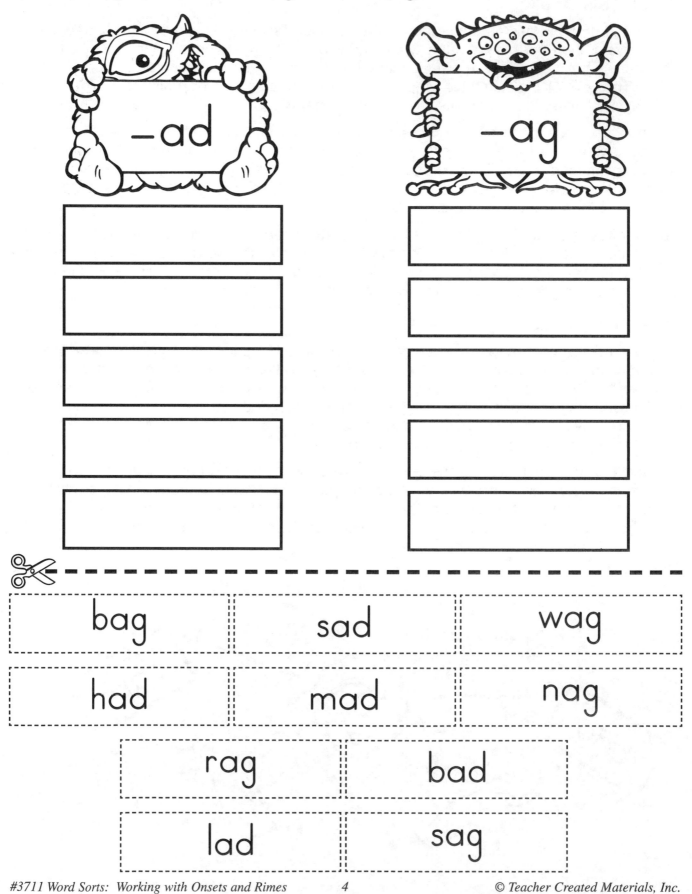

-ad

-ag

bag

sad

wag

had

mad

nag

rag

bad

lad

sag

Directions: Cut out the words below. Then sort the words so that all the *–ab* words are together and all the *–ack* words are together.

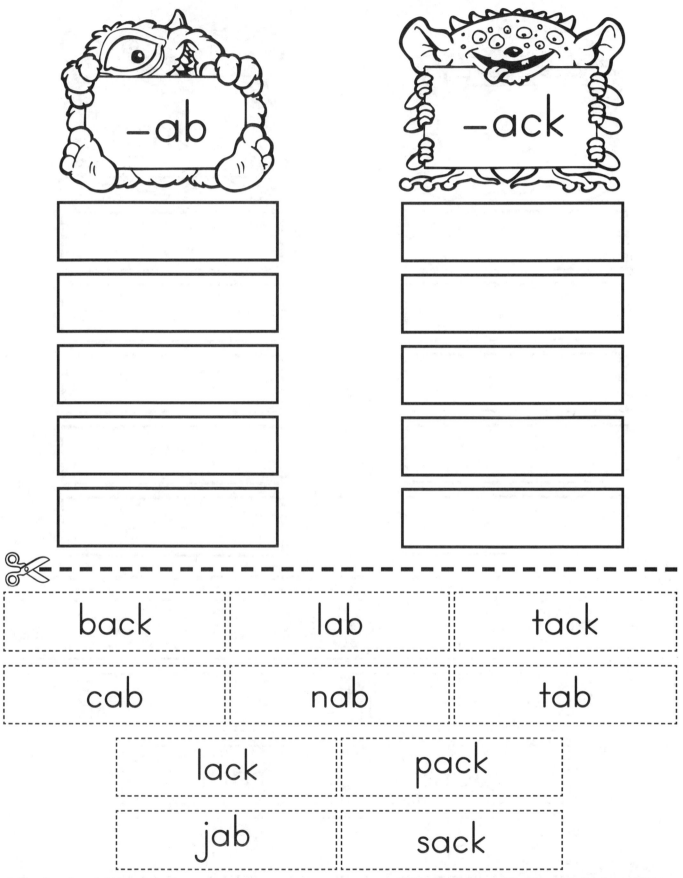

-ab

-ack

| back | lab | tack |
| cab | nab | tab |

| lack | pack |
| jab | sack |

Directions: Cut out the words below. Then sort the words so that all the *–am* words are together and all the *–amp* words are together.

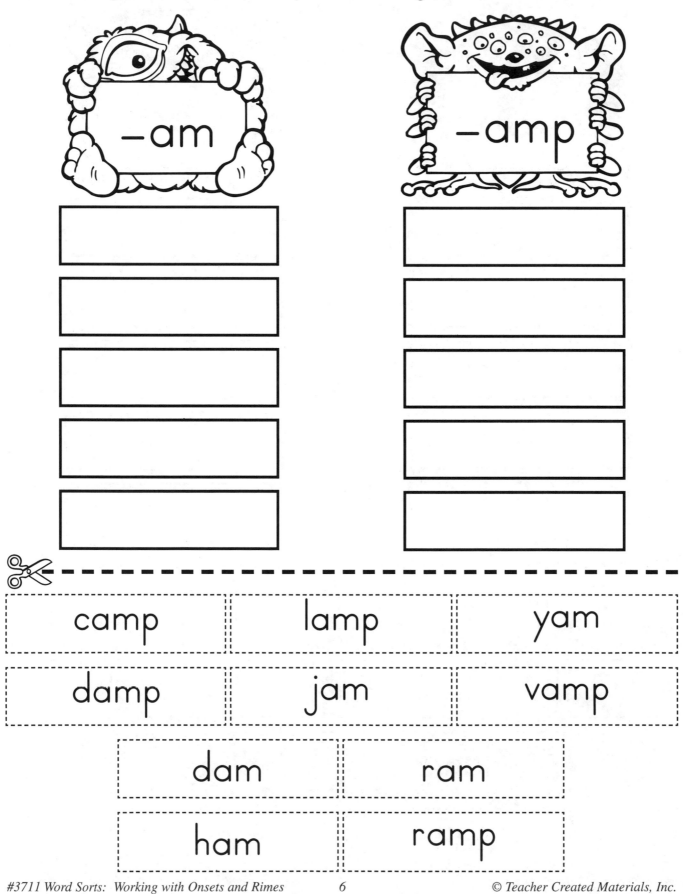

-am

-amp

| camp | lamp | yam |
| damp | jam | vamp |

| dam | ram |
| ham | ramp |

Directions: Cut out the words below. Then sort the words so that all the –*an* words are together and all the –*and* words are together.

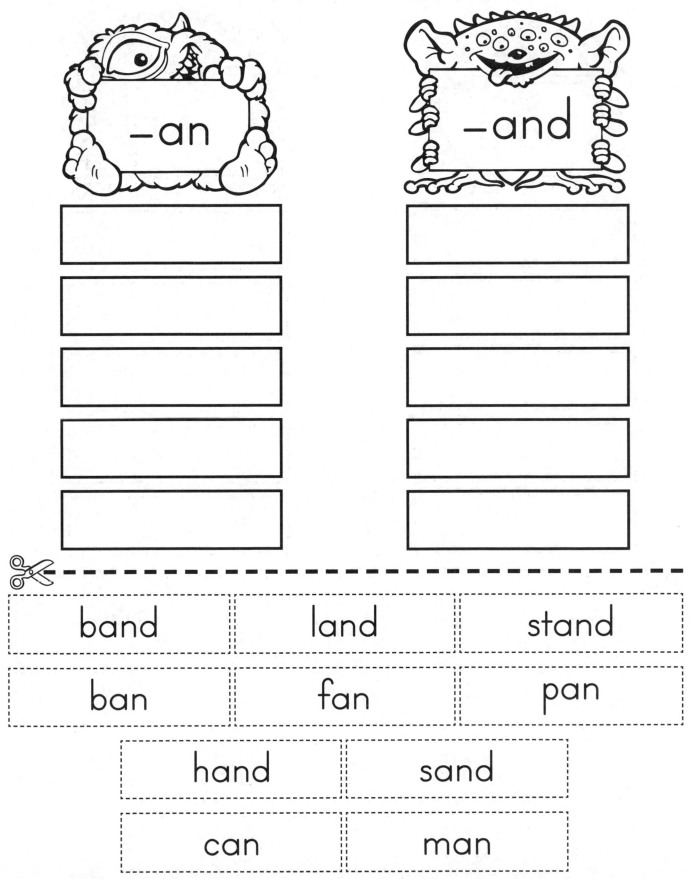

-an

-and

✂ --

| band | land | stand |

| ban | fan | pan |

| hand | sand |

| can | man |

Directions: Cut out the words below. Then sort the words so that all the *–ap* words are together and all the *–at* words are together.

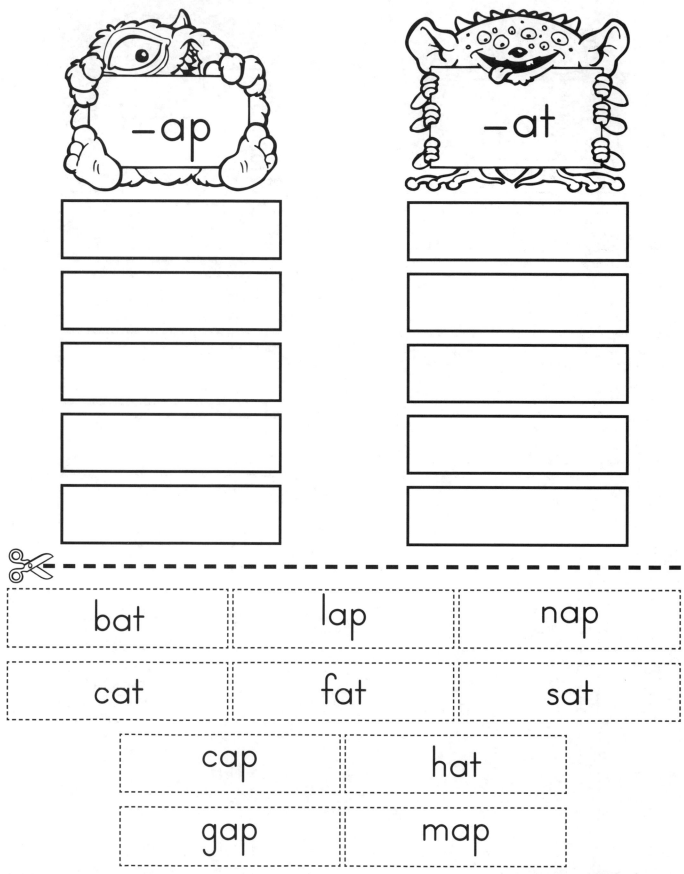

bat	lap	nap
cat	fat	sat

cap	hat
gap	map

Single Letter Onsets with Long a Rimes

Directions: Cut out the words below. Then sort the words so that all the *–ace* words are together and all the *–ail* words are together.

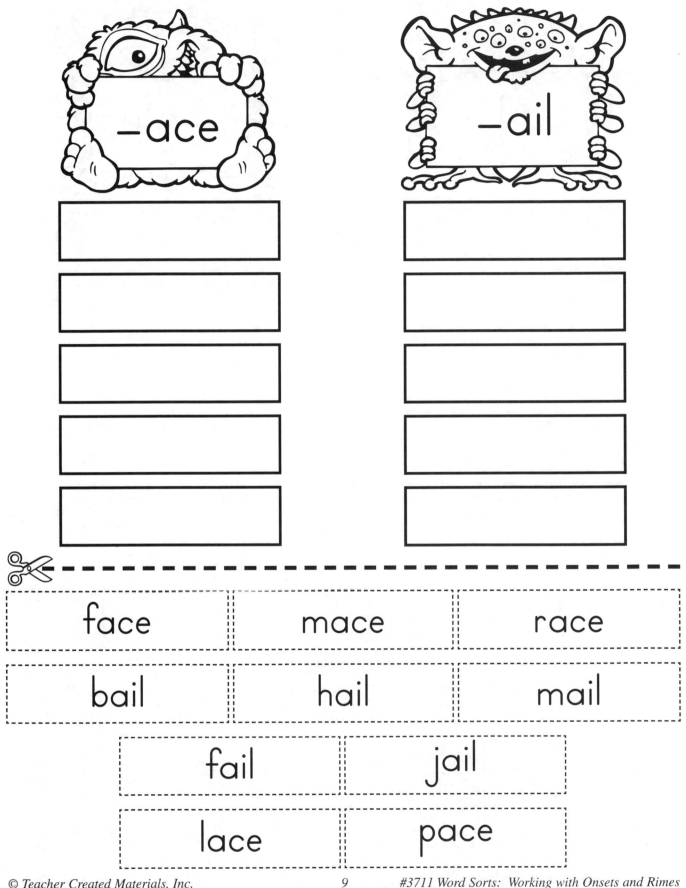

-ace

-ail

| face | mace | race |

| bail | hail | mail |

| fail | jail |

| lace | pace |

Single Letter Onsets with Long a Rimes

Directions: Cut out the words below. Then sort the words so that all the *–ake* words are together and all the *–ale* words are together.

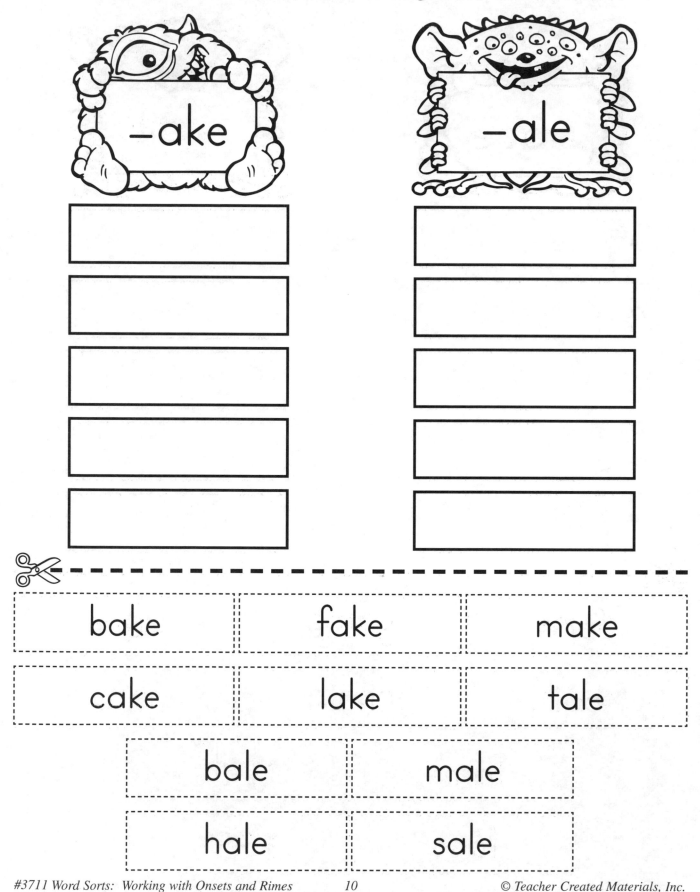

-ake

-ale

| bake | fake | make |
| cake | lake | tale |

| bale | male |
| hale | sale |

Directions: Cut out the words below. Then sort the words so that all the *–ame* words are together and all the *–ane* words are together.

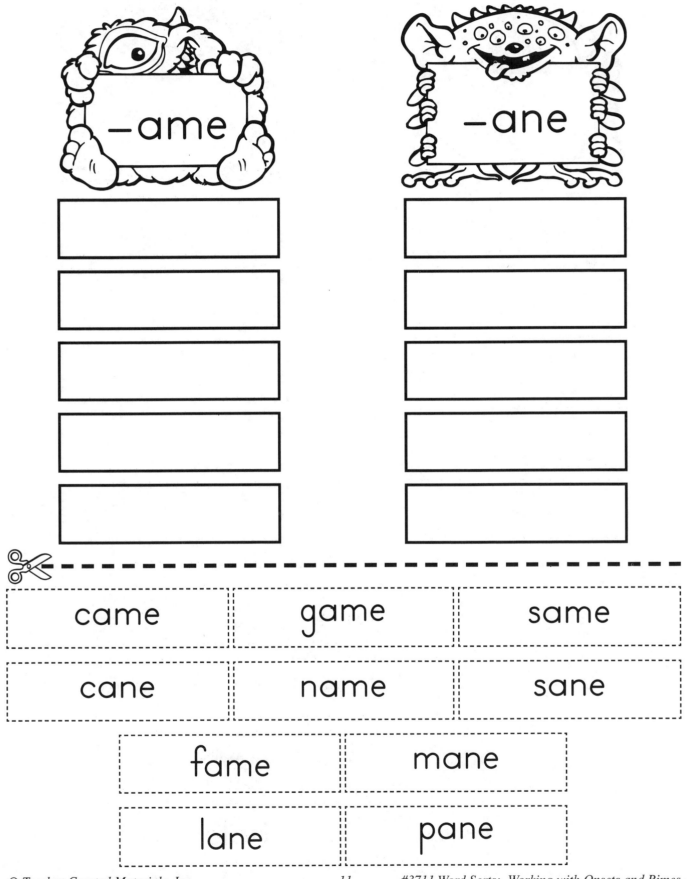

–ame

–ane

came	game	same
cane	name	sane

fame	mane
lane	pane

Single Letter Onsets with Long a Rimes

Directions: Cut out the words below. Then sort the words so that all the *–ate* words are together and all the *–ave* words are together.

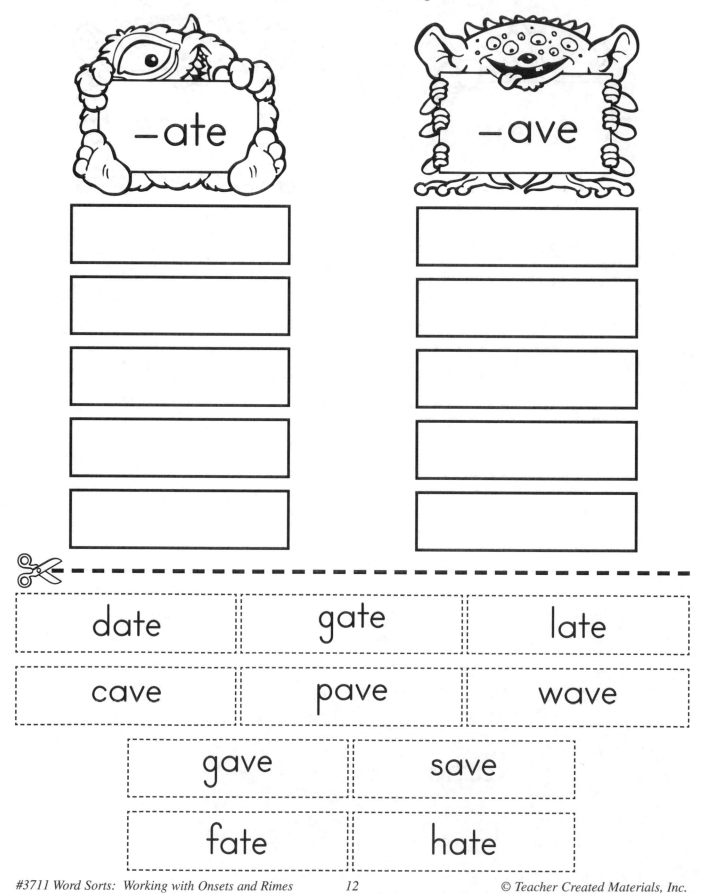

-ate

-ave

date   gate   late

cave   pave   wave

gave   save

fate   hate

Directions: Cut out the words below. Then sort the words so that all the *–ay* words are together and all the *–aze* words are together.

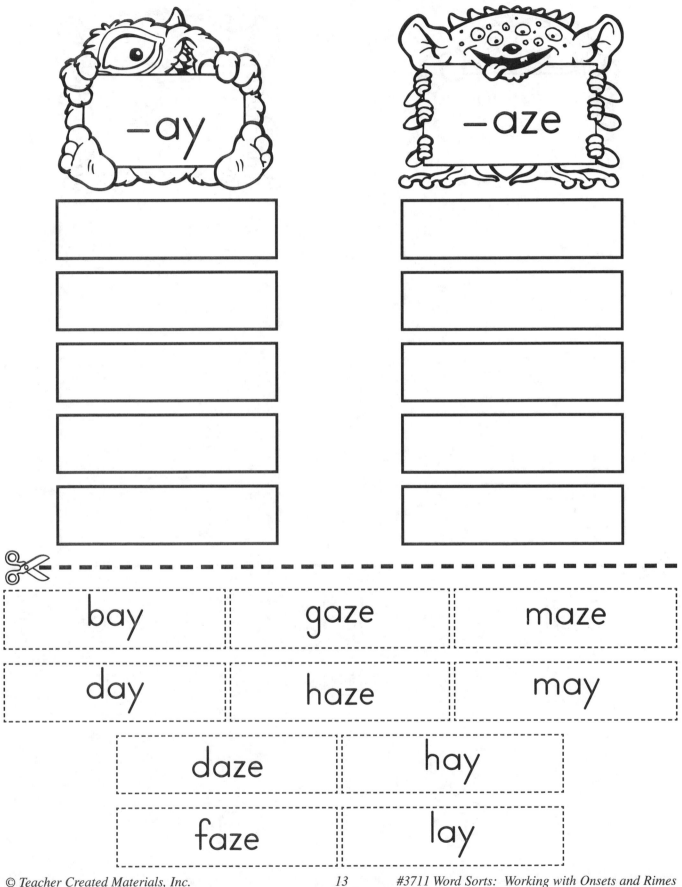

-ay

-aze

bay	gaze	maze
day	haze	may

daze	hay
faze	lay

Directions: Cut out the words below. Then sort the words so that all the *–ed* words are together and all the *–ell* words are together.

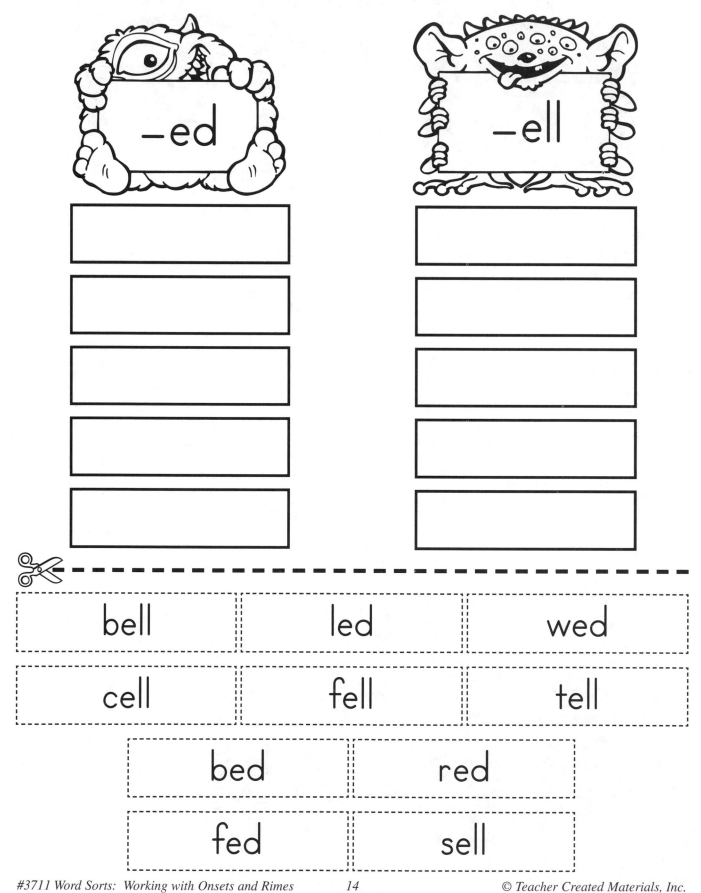

–ed

–ell

| bell | led | wed |
| cell | fell | tell |

| bed | red |
| fed | sell |

Single Letter Onsets Short e Rimes

Directions: Cut out the words below. Then sort the words so that all the *–en* words are together and all the *–end* words are together.

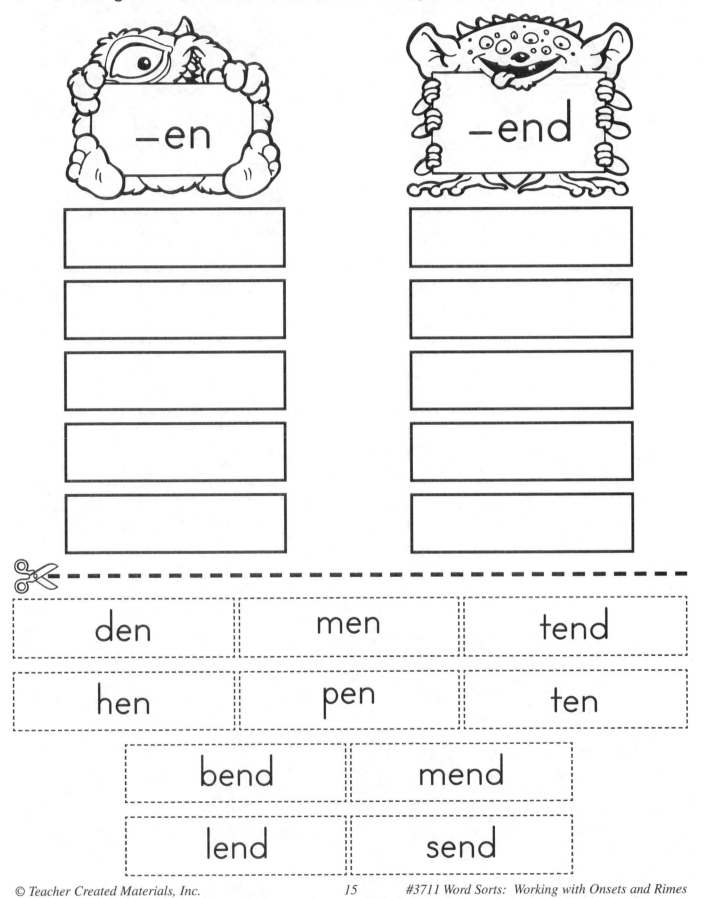

–en

–end

den   men   tend

hen   pen   ten

bend   mend

lend   send

Single Letter Onsets Short e Rimes

Directions: Cut out the words below. Then sort the words so that all the *–ent* words are together and all the *–est* words are together.

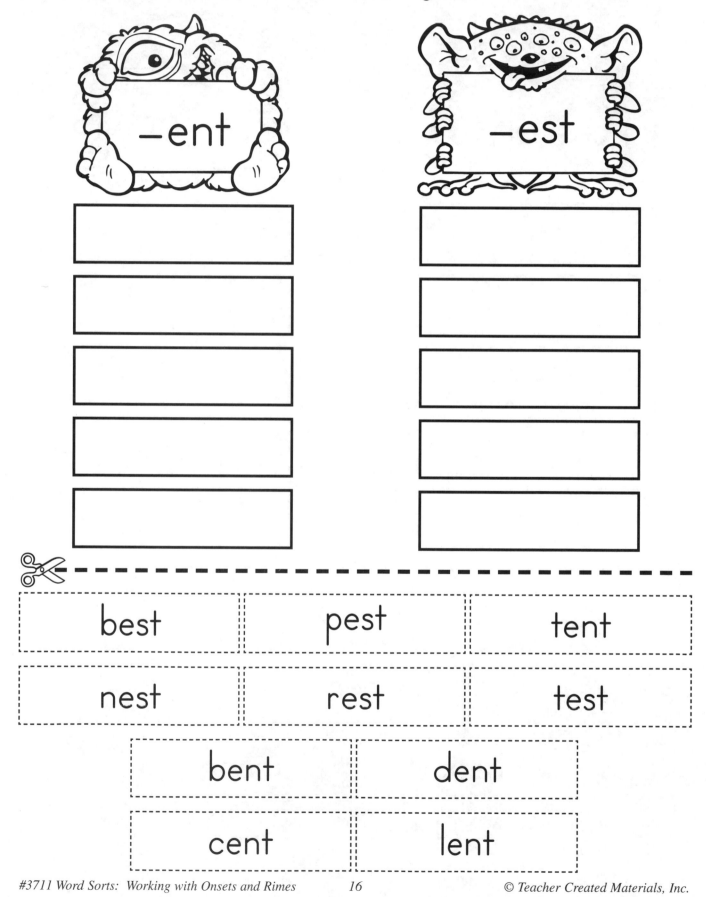

-ent

-est

best	pest	tent
nest	rest	test

bent	dent
cent	lent

Directions: Cut out the words below. Then sort the words so that all the *–et* words are together and all the *–elt* words are together.

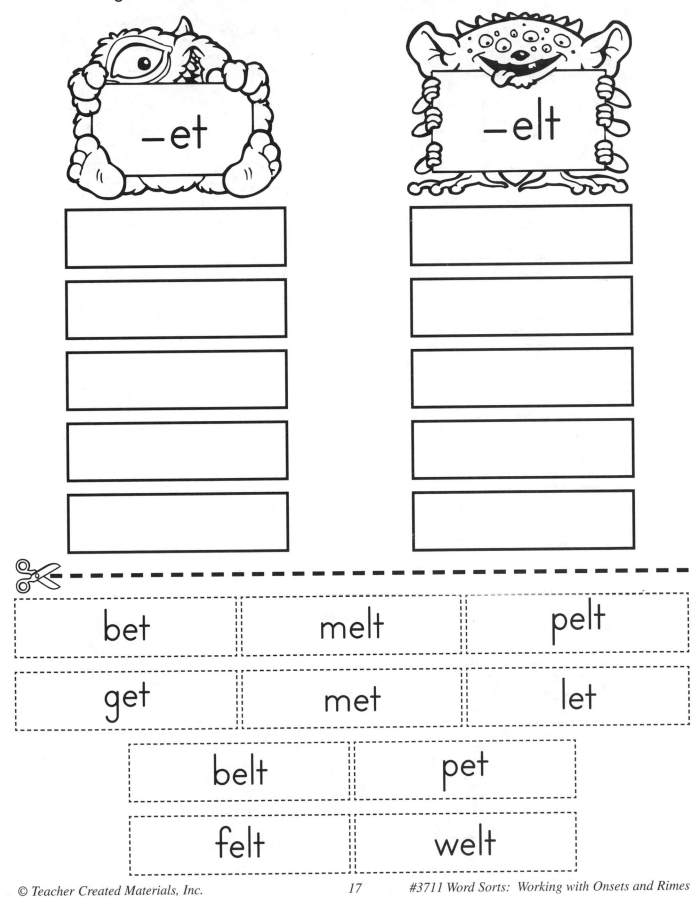

-et

-elt

| bet | melt | pelt |
| get | met | let |

| belt | pet |
| felt | welt |

Single Letter Onsets with Long e Rimes

Directions: Cut out the words below. Then sort the words so that all the *–eak* words are together and all the *–eal* words are together.

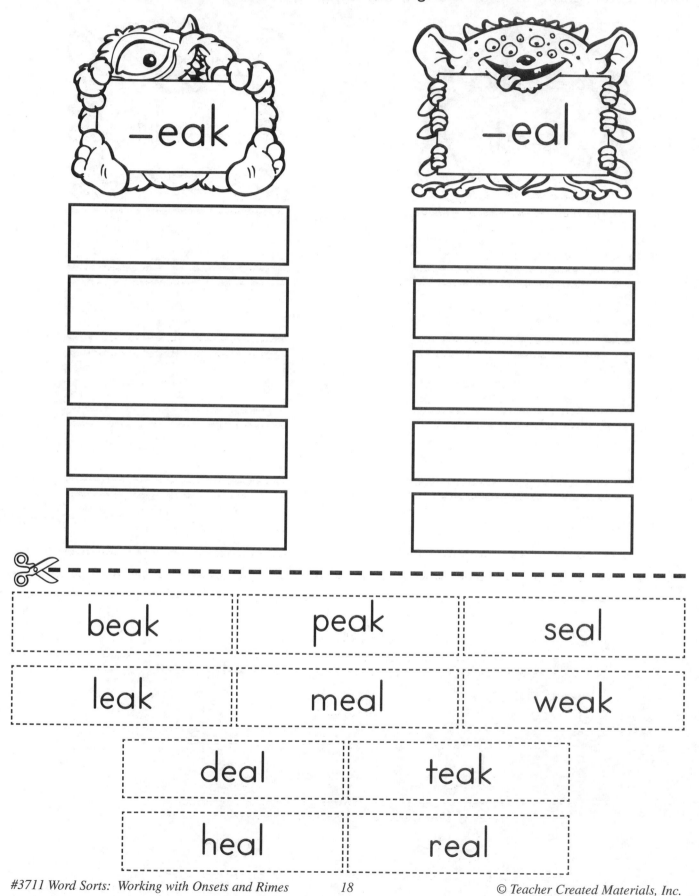

-eak

-eal

beak	peak	seal
leak	meal	weak
deal	teak
heal	real

Directions: Cut out the words below. Then sort the words so that all the *–ear* words are together and all the *–eat* words are together.

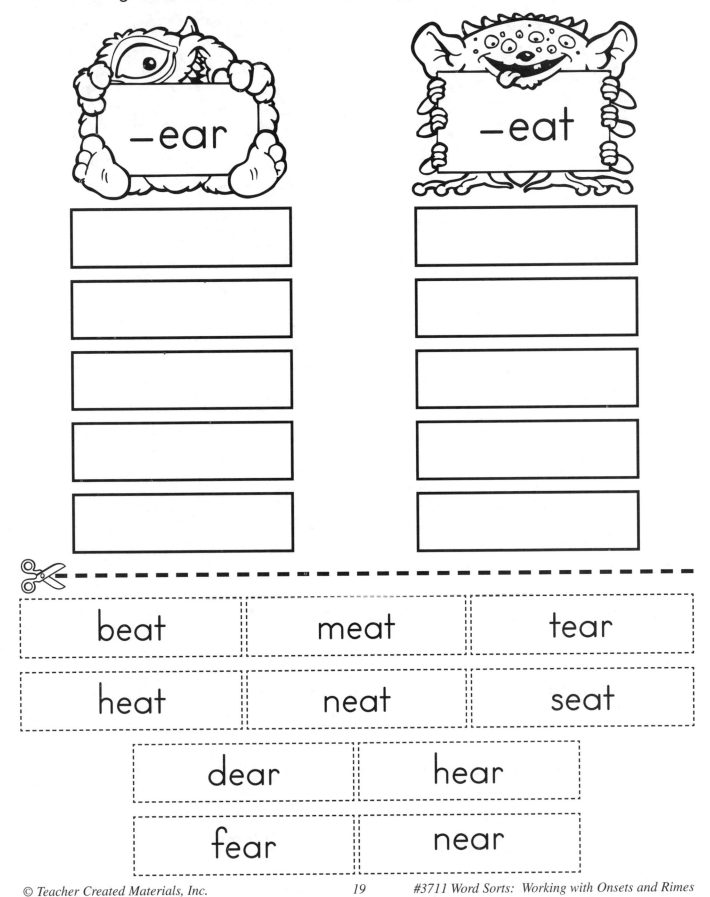

-ear

-eat

beat	meat	tear

heat	neat	seat

dear	hear

fear	near

Directions: Cut out the words below. Then sort the words so that all the *–ee* words are together and all the *–eed* words are together.

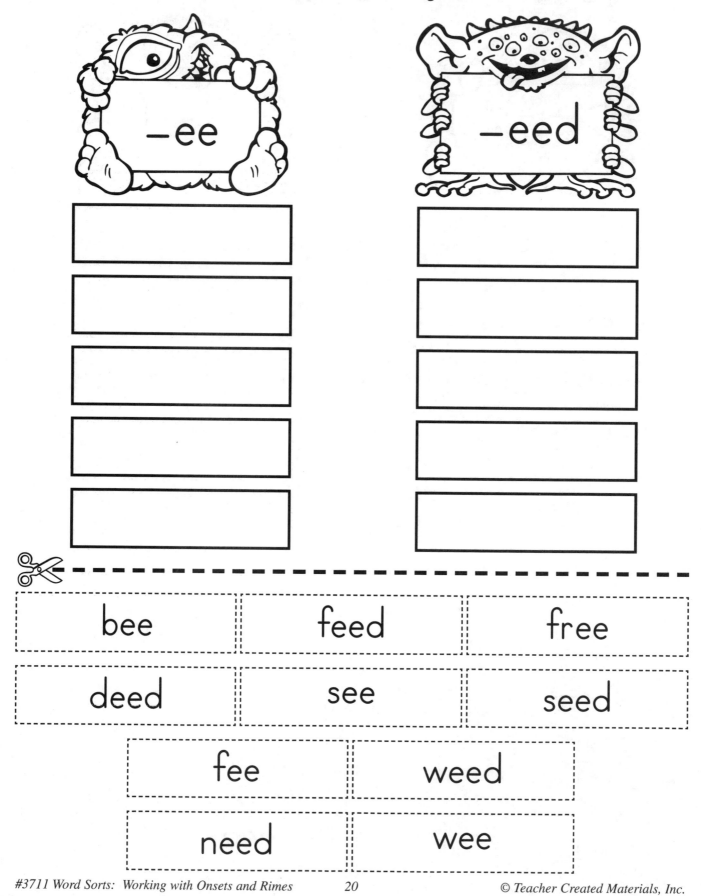

-ee

-eed

bee	feed	free
deed	see	seed
fee	weed	
need	wee	

Single Letter Onsets with Long e Rimes

Directions: Cut out the words below. Then sort the words so that all the *–eek* words are together and all the *–eel* words are together.

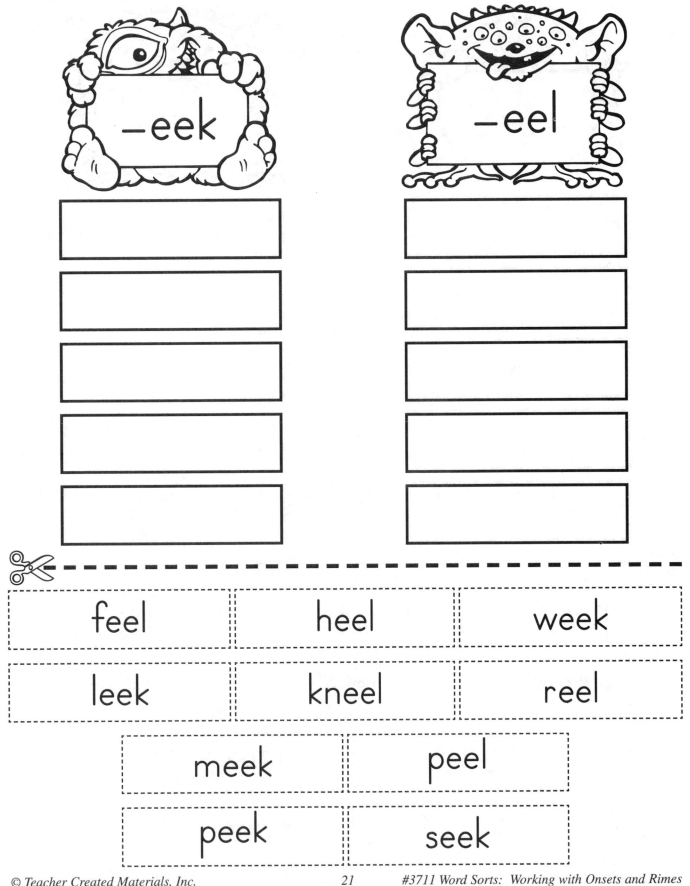

–eek

–eel

| feel | heel | week |

| leek | kneel | reel |

| meek | peel |

| peek | seek |

Directions: Cut out the words below. Then sort the words so that all the *–eep* words are together and all the *–eer* words are together.

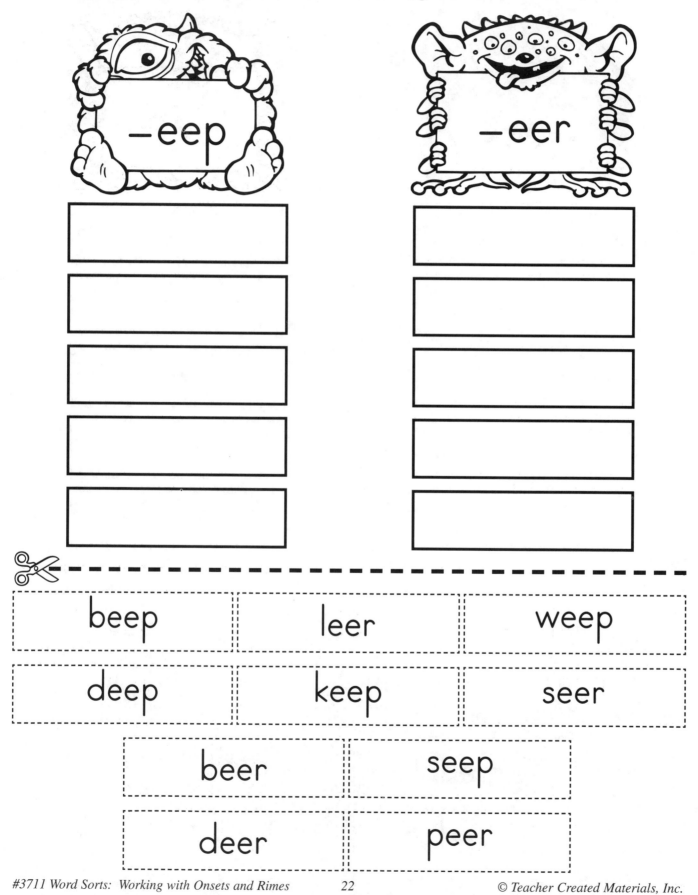

–eep

–eer

beep	leer	weep

deep	keep	seer

beer	seep

deer	peer

Directions: Cut out the words below. Then sort the words so that all the *–ick* words are together and all the *–id* words are together.

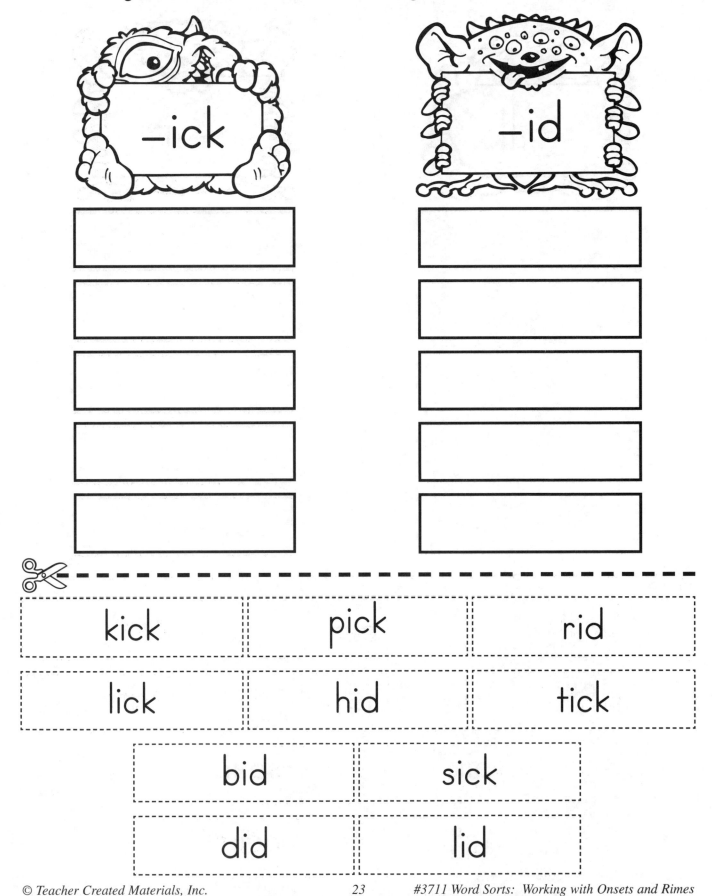

–ick	–id

kick	pick	rid
lick	hid	tick

bid	sick
did	lid

Directions: Cut out the words below. Then sort the words so that all the *–ill* words are together and all the *–in* words are together.

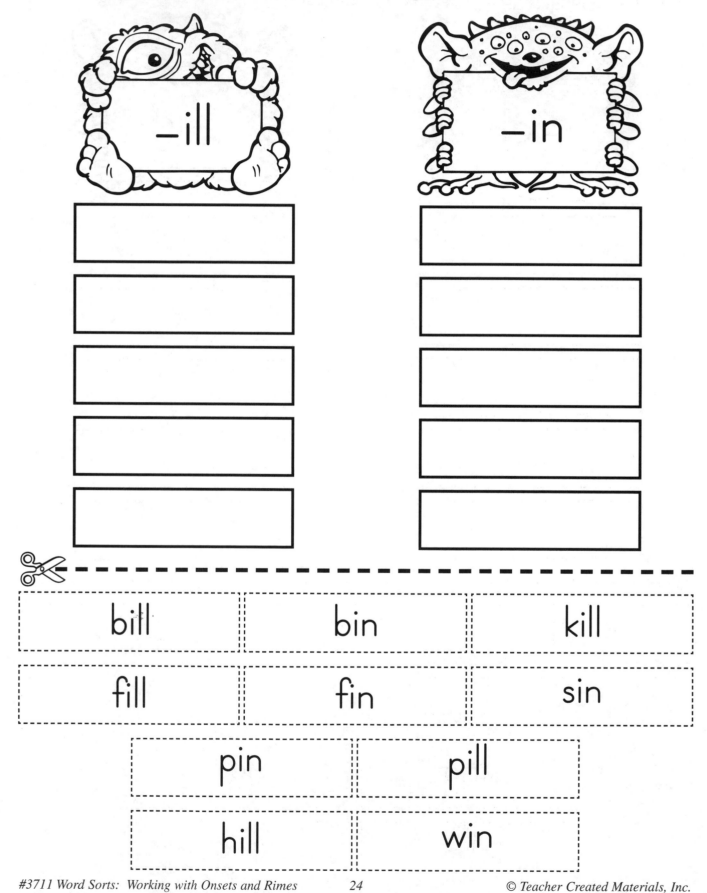

–ill

–in

bill

bin

kill

fill

fin

sin

pin

pill

hill

win

Single Letter Onsets with Short i Rimes

Directions: Cut out the words below. Then sort the words so that all the *–ing* words are together and all the *–ink* words are together.

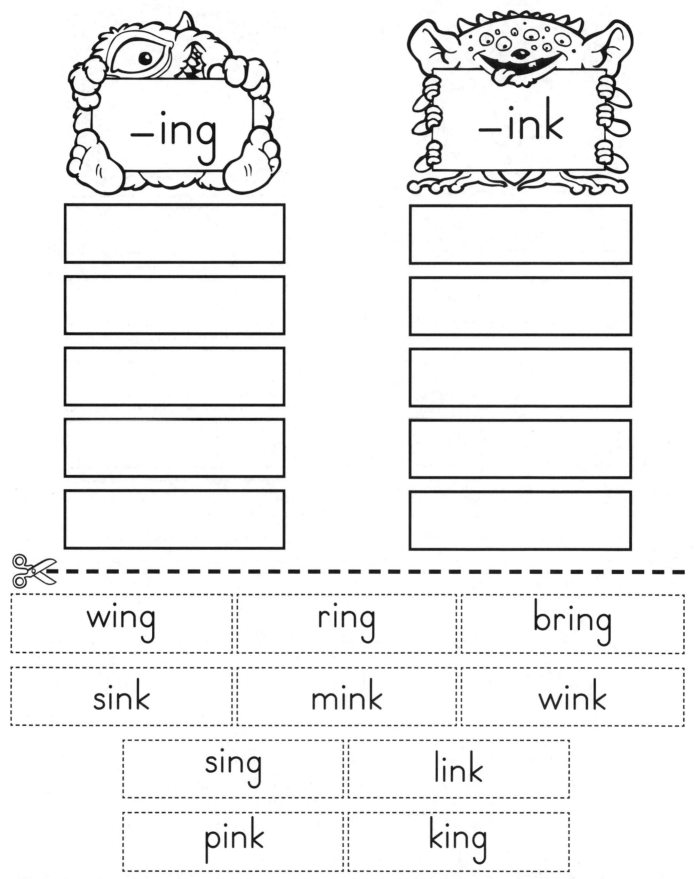

–ing

–ink

wing	ring	bring
sink	mink	wink

sing	link
pink	king

Directions: Cut out the words below. Then sort the words so that all the *–ip* words are together and all the *–it* words are together.

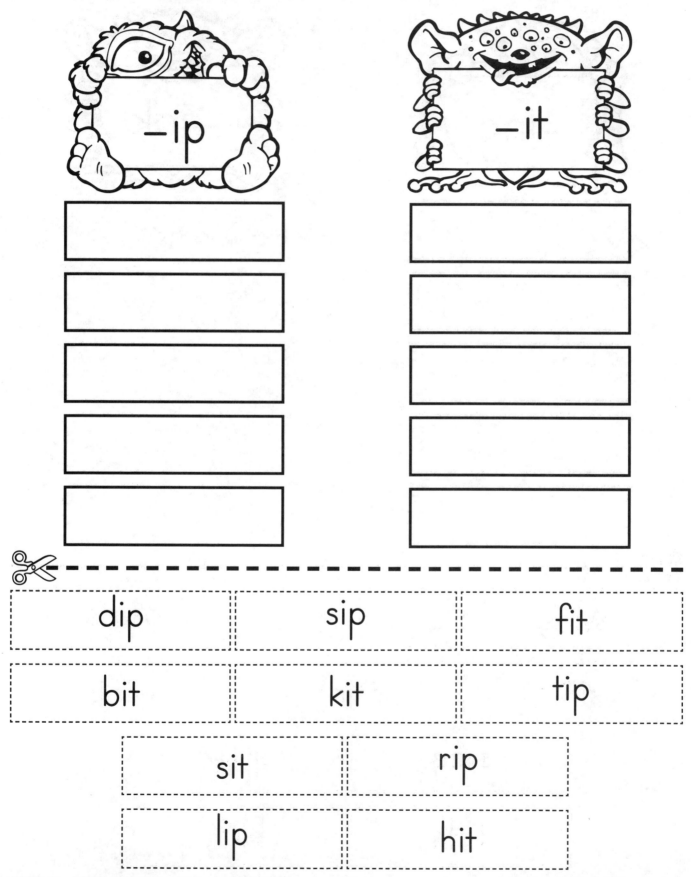

-ip

-it

✂ ------------------------------

dip	sip	fit
bit	kit	tip

sit	rip
lip	hit

Single Letter Onsets with Long i Rimes

Directions: Cut out the words below. Then sort the words so that all the *–ice* words are together and all the *–ide* words are together.

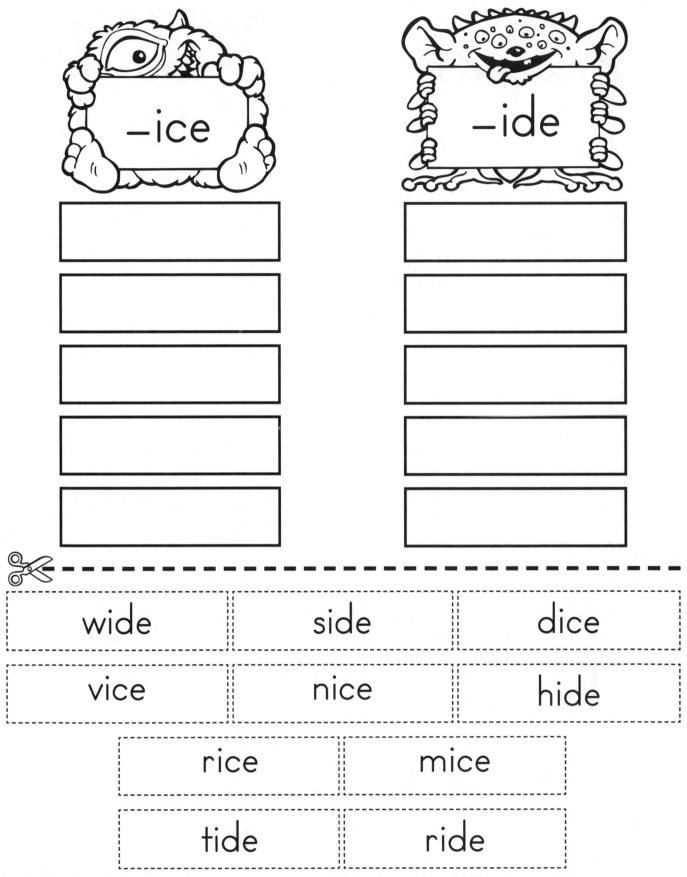

–ice	–ide

wide	side	dice
vice	nice	hide

rice	mice
tide	ride

Directions: Cut out the words below. Then sort the words so that all the *–ie* words are together and all the *–ight* words are together.

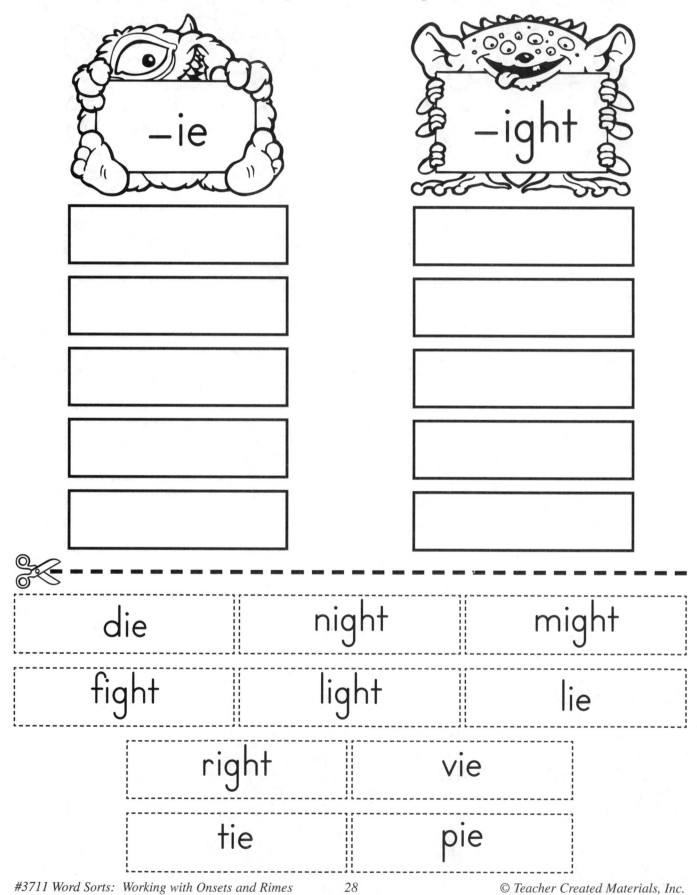

-ie

-ight

die	night	might
fight	light	lie
right	vie
tie	pie

Directions: Cut out the words below. Then sort the words so that all the *–ike* words are together and all the *–ile* words are together.

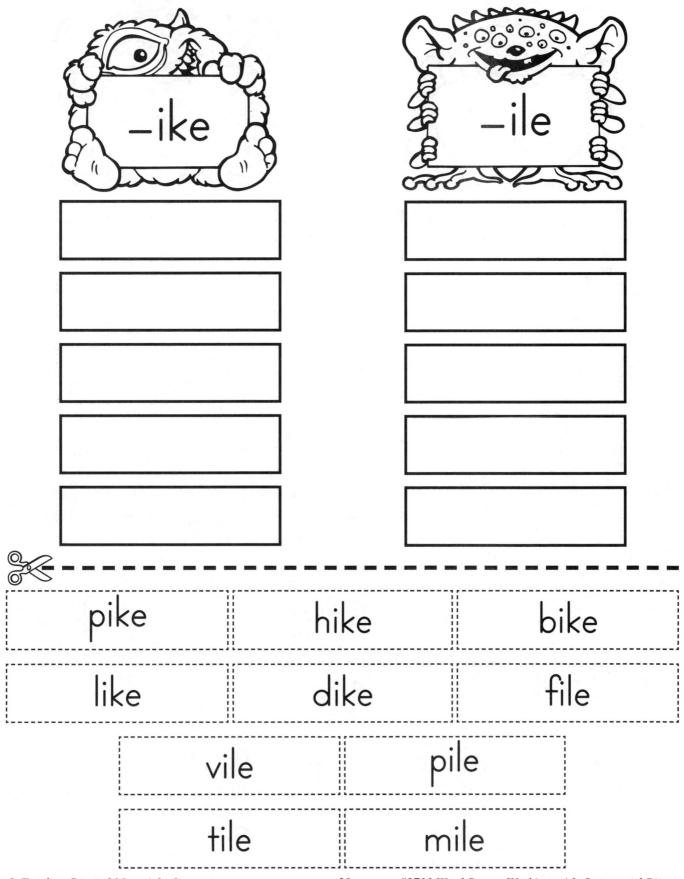

–ike

–ile

| pike | hike | bike |
| like | dike | file |

| vile | pile |
| tile | mile |

Directions: Cut out the words below. Then sort the words so that all the –*ind* words are together and all the –*ine* words are together.

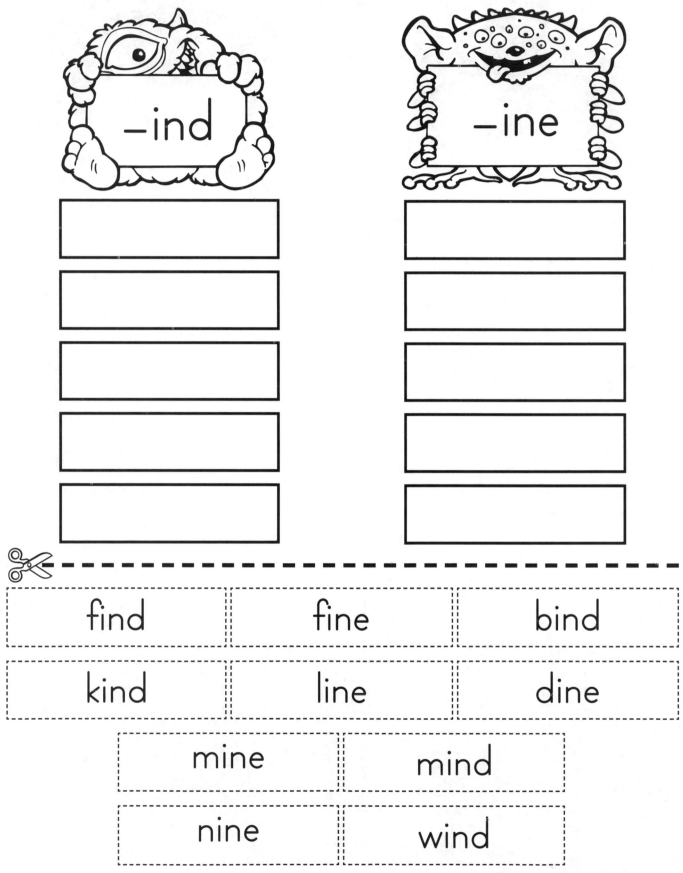

–ind

–ine

find	fine	bind
kind	line	dine
mine	mind
nine	wind

Directions: Cut out the words below. Then sort the words so that all the *–ob* words are together and all the *–ock* words are together.

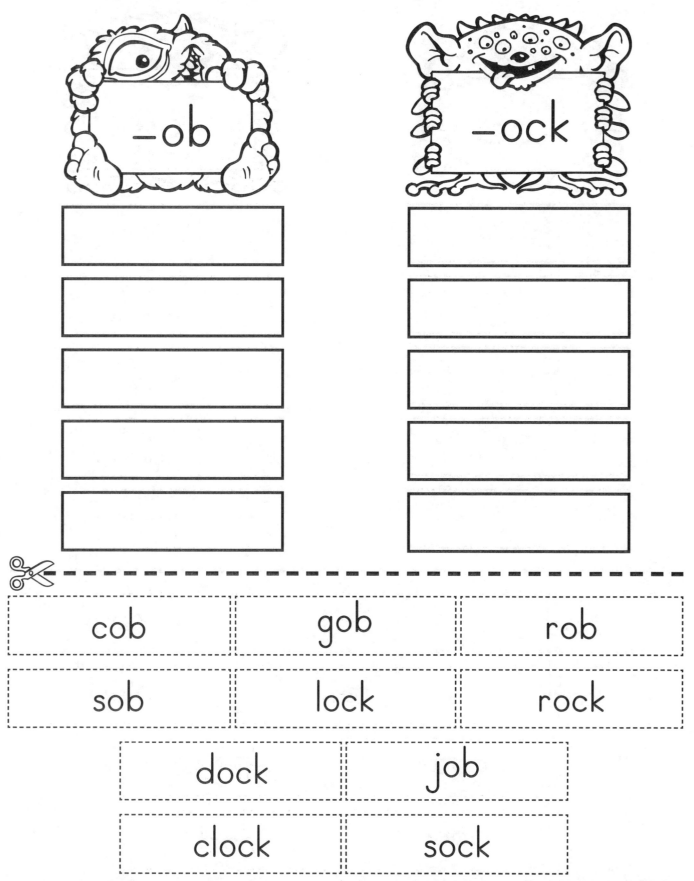

-ob

-ock

cob	gob	rob
sob	lock	rock

dock	job
clock	sock

Directions: Cut out the words below. Then sort the words so that all the *–od* words are together and all the *–og* words are together.

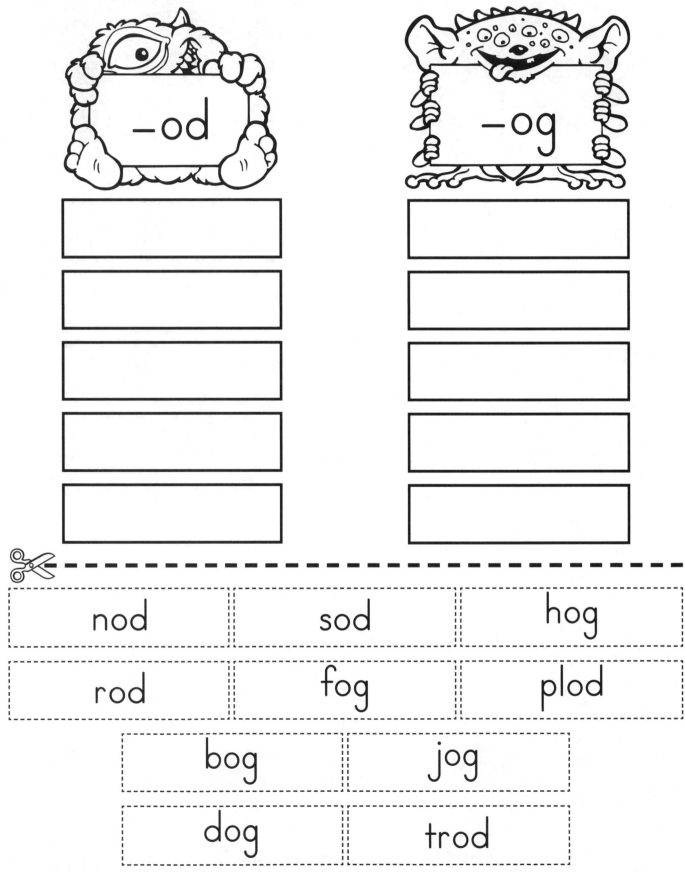

-od

-og

nod   sod   hog

rod   fog   plod

bog   jog

dog   trod

Single Letter Onsets with Short o Rimes

Directions: Cut out the words below. Then sort the words so that all the –op words are together and all the –ot words are together.

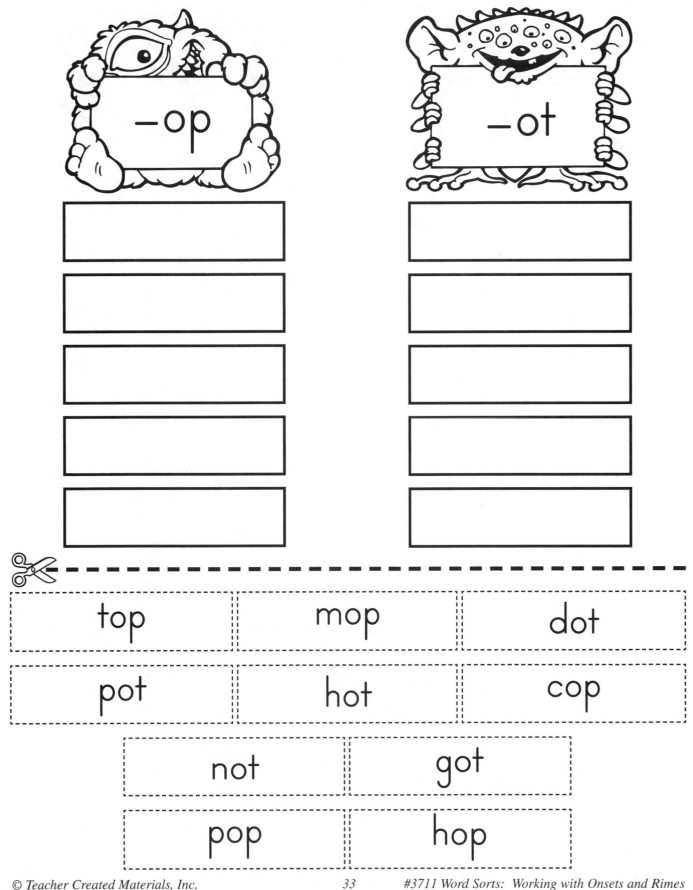

-op

-ot

| top | mop | dot |
| pot | hot | cop |

| not | got |
| pop | hop |

Single Letter Onsets with Long o Rimes

Directions: Cut out the words below. Then sort the words so that all the *–old* words are together and all the *–one* words are together.

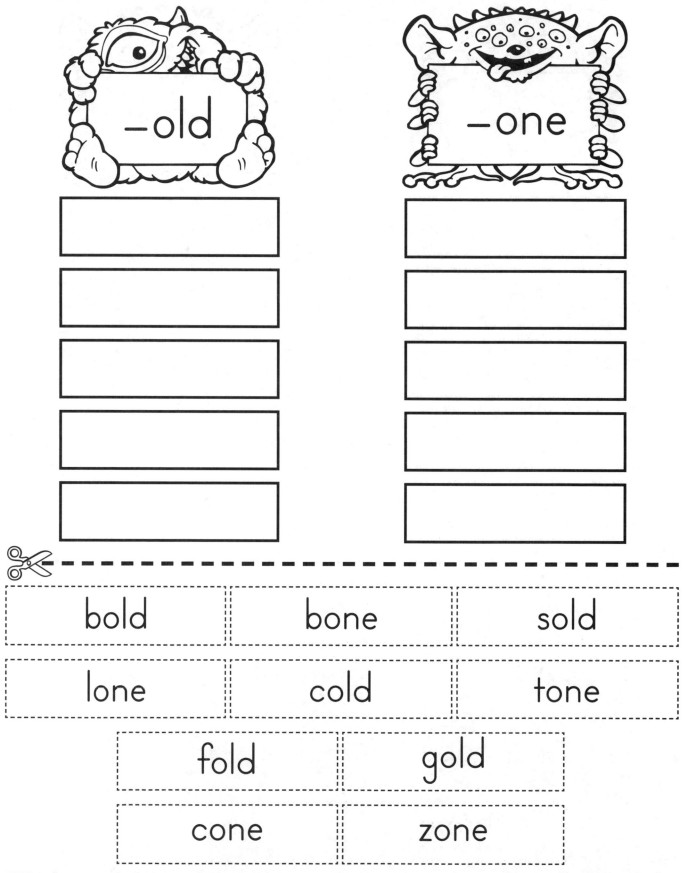

–old

–one

bold

bone

sold

lone

cold

tone

fold

gold

cone

zone

Single Letter Onsets with Long o Rimes

Directions: Cut out the words below. Then sort the words so that all the *–ope* words are together and all the *–ow* words are together.

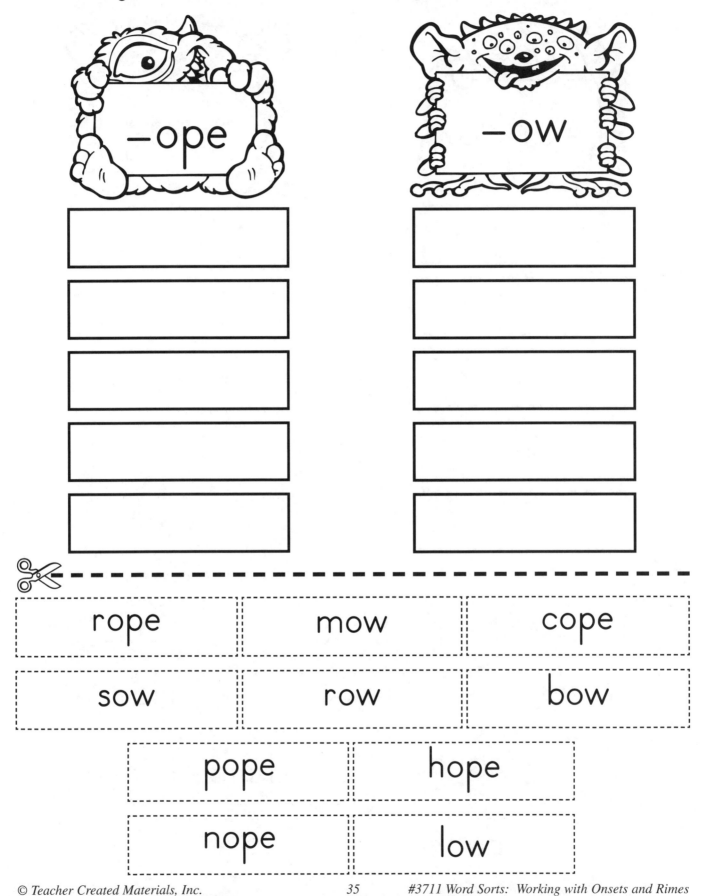

-ope

-ow

rope	mow	cope
sow	row	bow

pope   hope

nope   low

Directions: Cut out the words below. Then sort the words so that all the *–ance* words are together and all the *–ang* words are together.

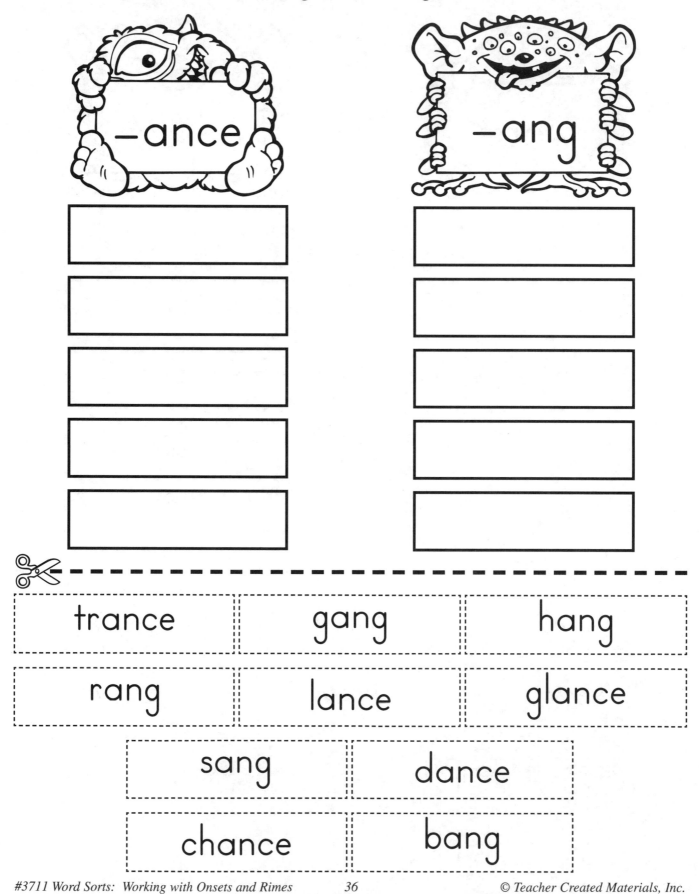

-ance

-ang

| trance | gang | hang |
| rang | lance | glance |

sang   dance

chance   bang

Directions: Cut out the words below. Then sort the words so that all the *–ank* words are together and all the *–ant* words are together.

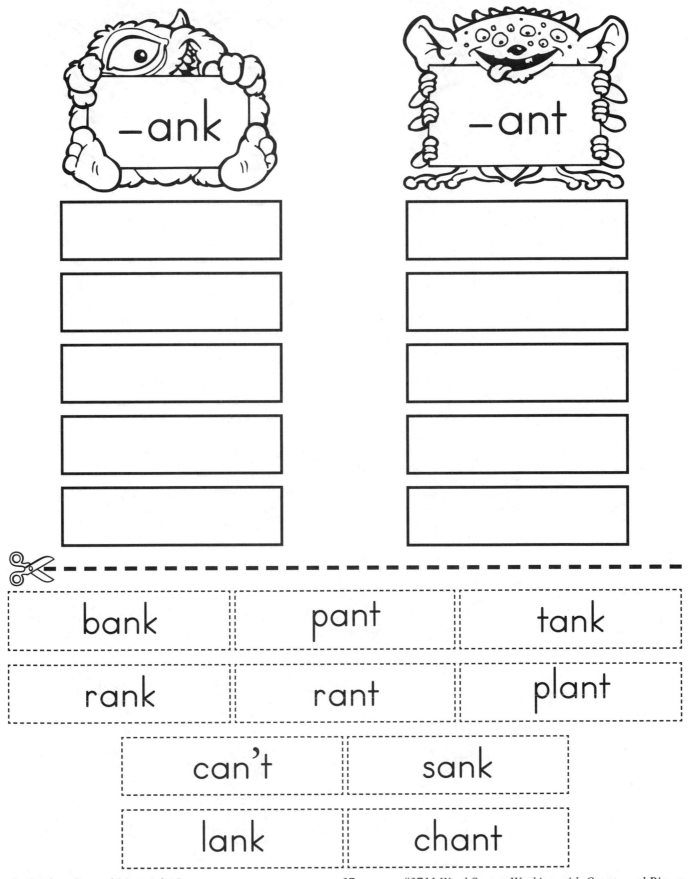

–ank	–ant

bank	pant	tank

rank	rant	plant

can't	sank

lank	chant

© *Teacher Created Materials, Inc.*   37

Directions: Cut out the words below. Then sort the words so that all the *–ash* words are together and all the *–ast* words are together.

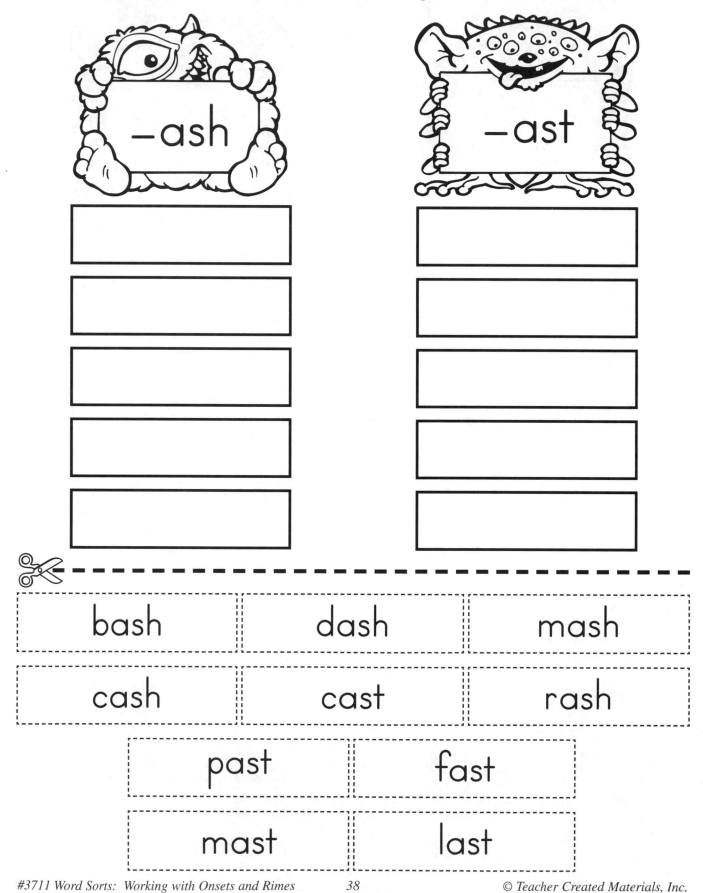

-ash

-ast

bash	dash	mash
cash	cast	rash

past	fast
mast	last

Directions: Cut out the words below. Then sort the words so that all the *–atch* words are together and all the *–ass* words are together.

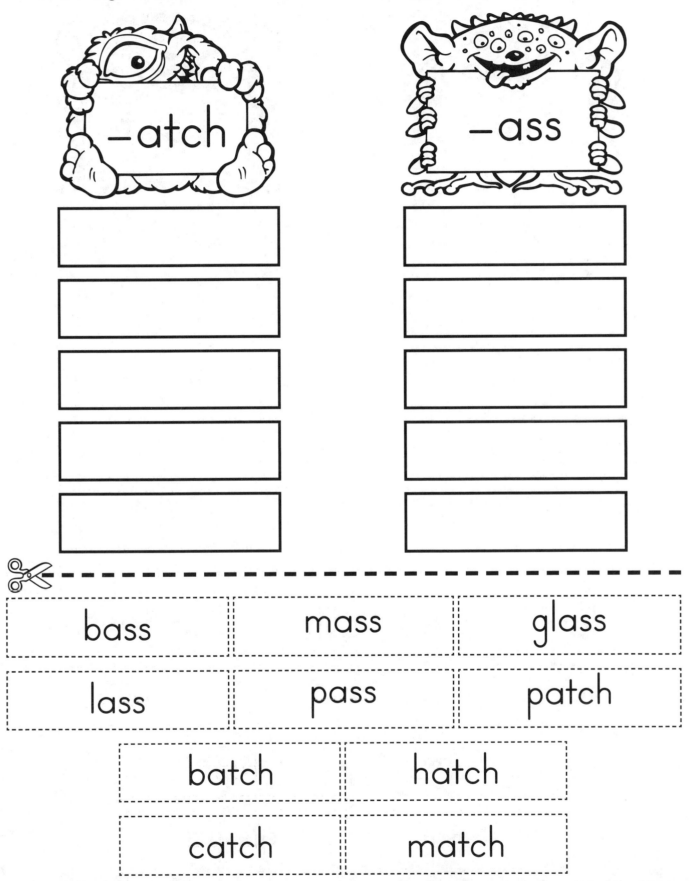

–atch

–ass

bass

mass

glass

lass

pass

patch

batch

hatch

catch

match

Blend & Single Letter Onsets with Long a Rimes

Directions: Cut out the words below. Then sort the words so that all the *–ain* words are together and all the *–ape* words are together.

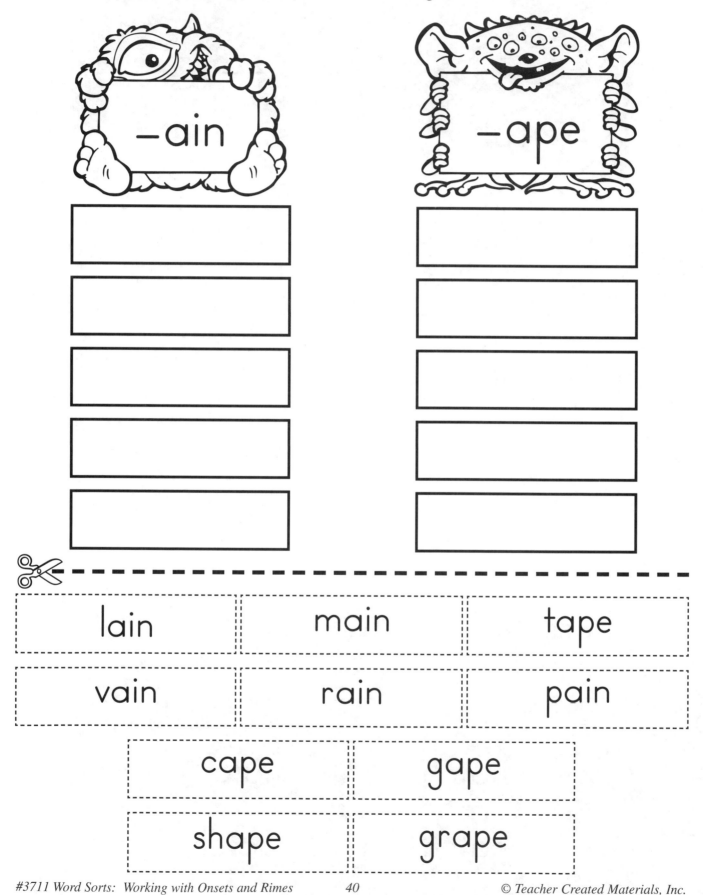

-ain

-ape

| lain | main | tape |
| vain | rain | pain |

| cape | gape |
| shape | grape |

Directions: Cut out the words below. Then sort the words so that all the *–ame* words are together and all the *–ane* words are together.

–ame

–ane

✂ -

| Jane | lane | name |
| blame | frame | plane |

| flame | shame |
| crane | cane |

Blend & Single Letter Onsets with Short e Rimes

Directions: Cut out the words below. Then sort the words so that all the –*eck* words are together and all the –*elt* words are together.

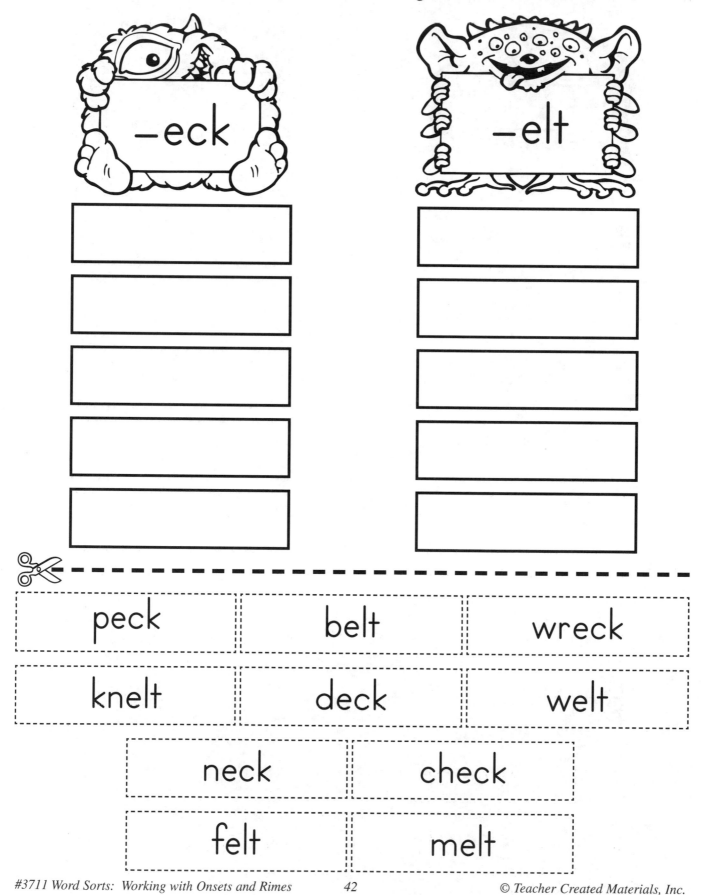

–eck

–elt

peck	belt
knelt	deck
neck	check
felt	melt

wreck

welt

Blend & Single Letter Onsets with Short e Rimes

Directions: Cut out the words below. Then sort the words so that all the *–ench* words are together and all the *–ess* words are together.

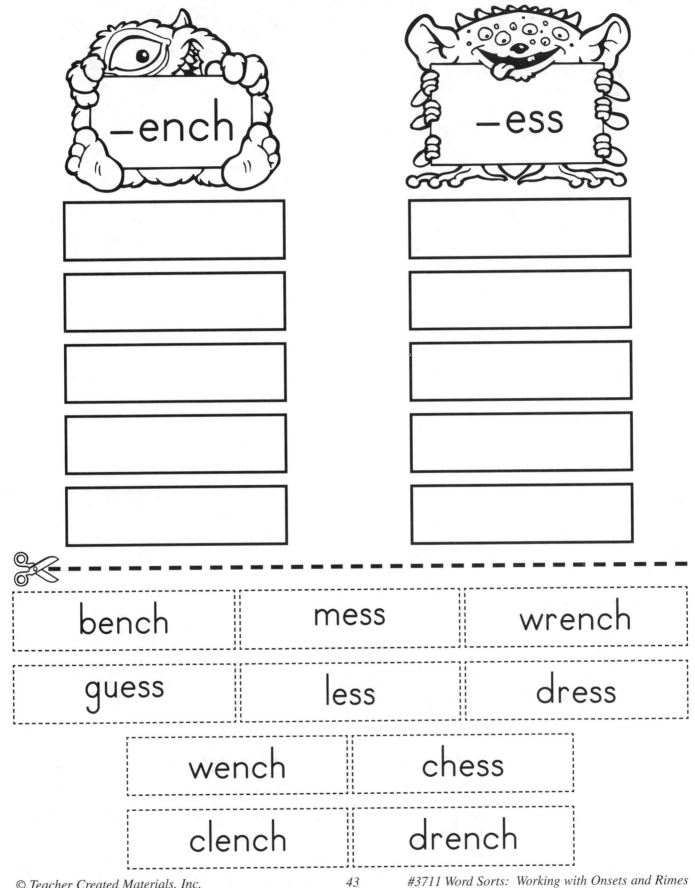

-ench

-ess

✂ -

bench	mess	wrench
guess	less	dress

wench	chess
clench	drench

Directions: Cut out the words below. Then sort the words so that all the *–each* words are together and all the *–eam* words are together.

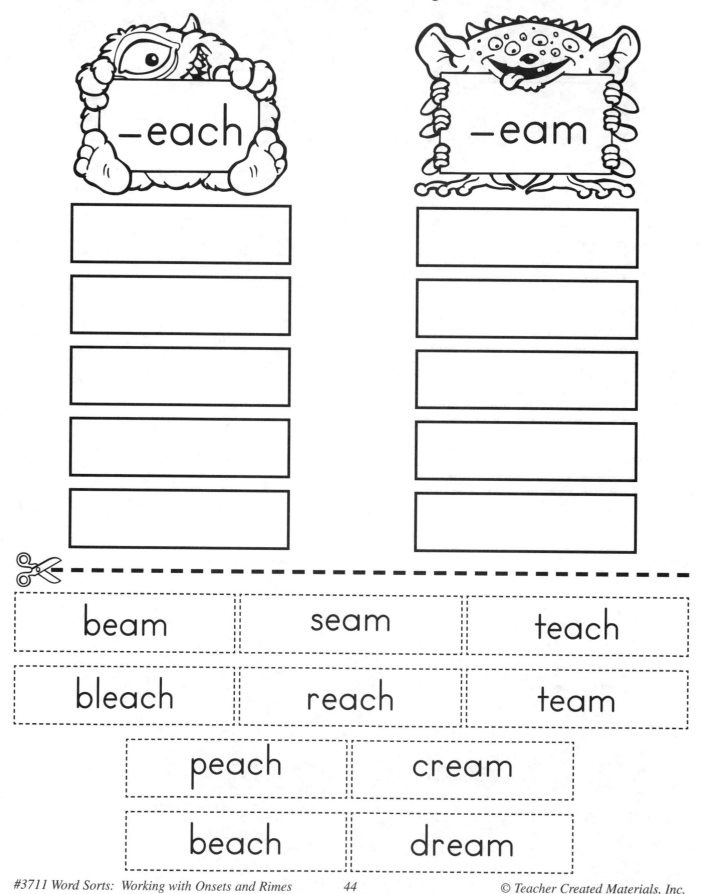

–each

–eam

beam	seam	teach
bleach	reach	team
peach	cream
beach	dream

Blend & Single Letter Onsets with Long e Rimes

Directions: Cut out the words below. Then sort the words so that all the *–ean* words are together and all the *–eet* words are together.

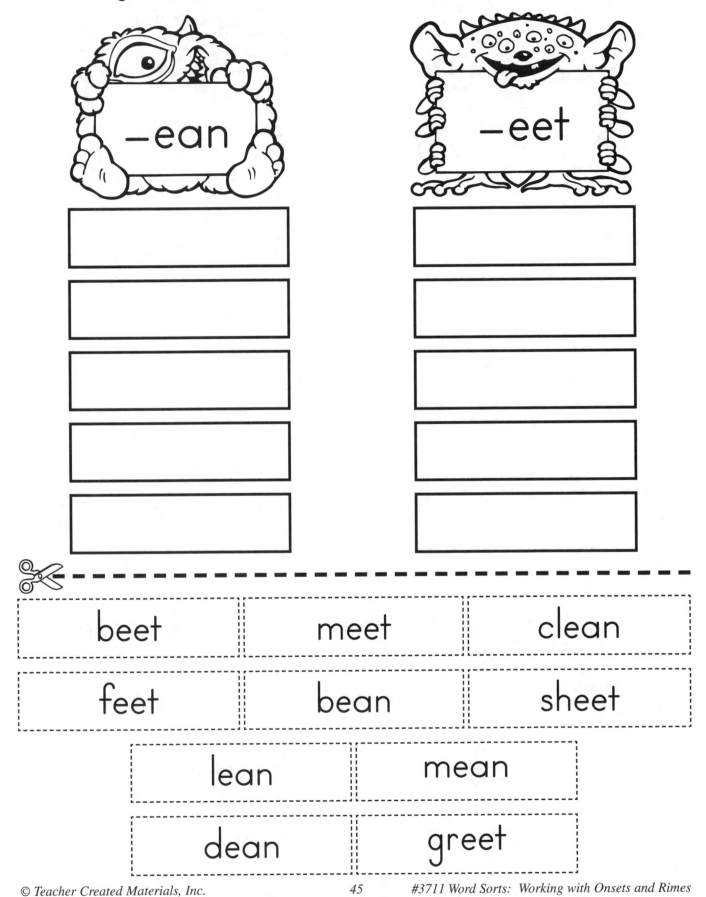

-ean

-eet

| beet | meet | clean |
| feet | bean | sheet |

| lean | mean |
| dean | greet |

Directions: Cut out the words below. Then sort the words so that all the *–een* words are together and all the *–eeze* words are together.

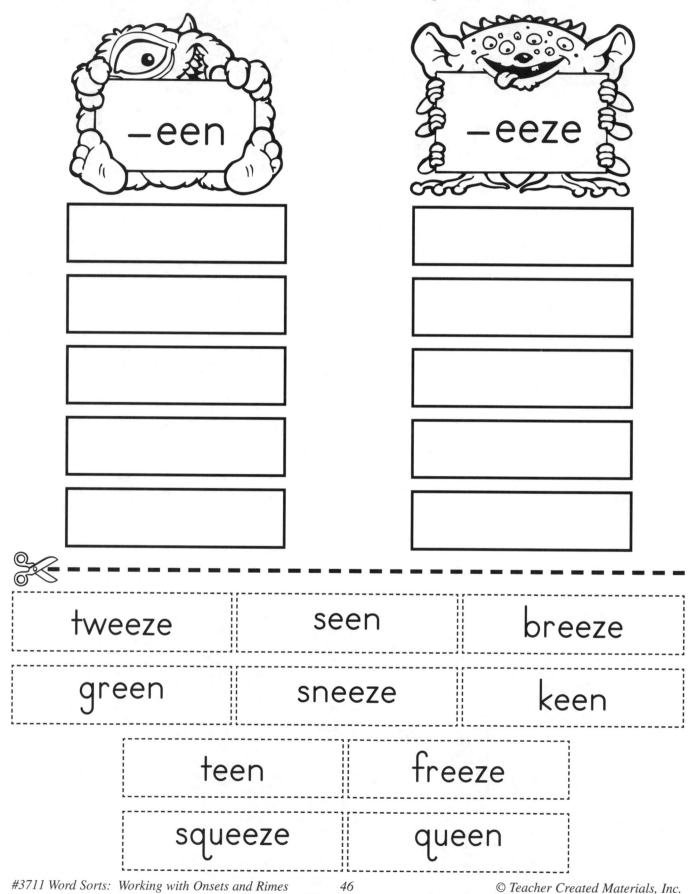

–een

–eeze

tweeze	seen	breeze
green	sneeze	keen

teen	freeze
squeeze	queen

Blend & Single Letter Onsets with Short i Rimes

Directions: Cut out the words below. Then sort the words so that all the *–ib* words are together and all the *–ift* words are together.

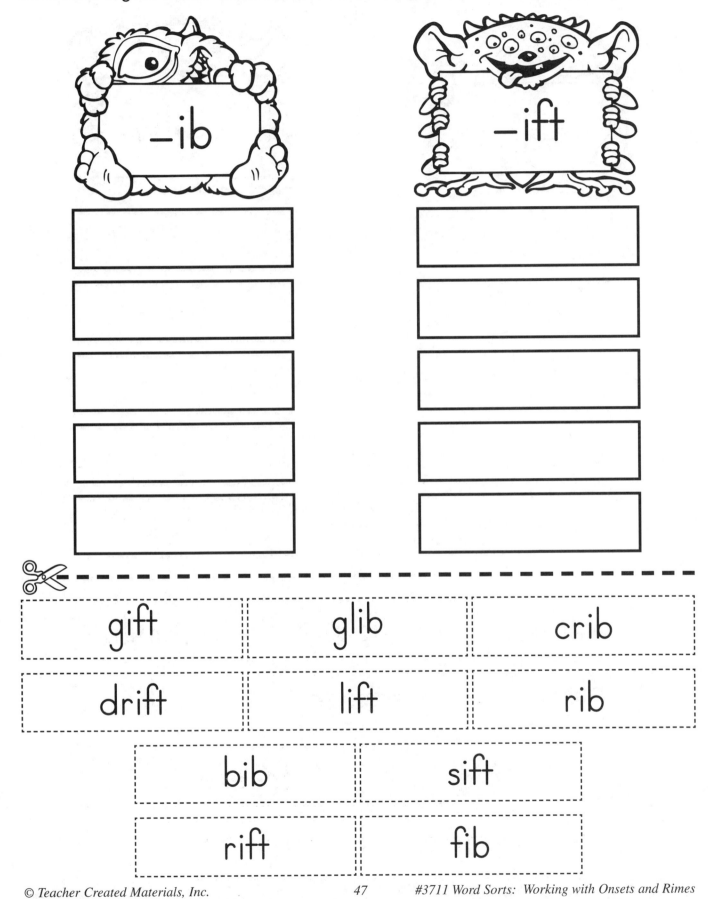

–ib

–ift

gift

glib

crib

drift

lift

rib

bib

sift

rift

fib

Directions: Cut out the words below. Then sort the words so that all the *–ig* words are together and all the *–ilt* words are together.

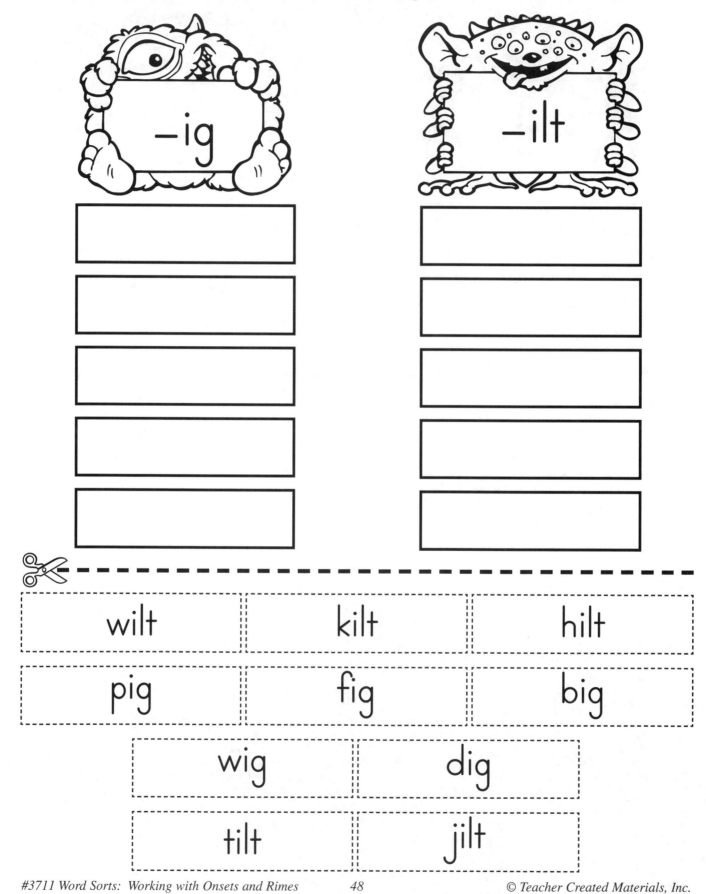

-ig

-ilt

| wilt | kilt | hilt |

| pig | fig | big |

| wig | dig |

| tilt | jilt |

Directions: Cut out the words below. Then sort the words so that all the *–im* words are together and all the *–inch* words are together.

-im

-inch

| cinch | him | grim |
| dim | pinch | winch |

| rim | clinch |
| finch | brim |

Blend & Single Letter Onsets with Short i Rimes

Directions: Cut out the words below. Then sort the words so that all the *–isk* words are together and all the *–iss* words are together.

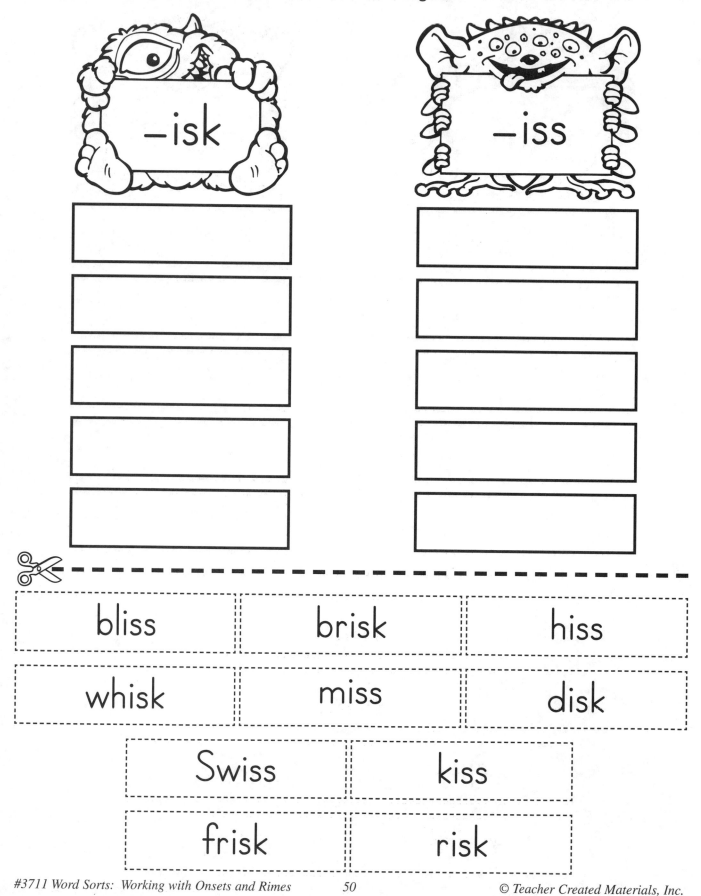

−isk

−iss

bliss	brisk	hiss
whisk	miss	disk

Swiss   kiss

frisk   risk

Directions: Cut out the words below. Then sort the words so that all the *–ist* words are together and all the *–int* words are together.

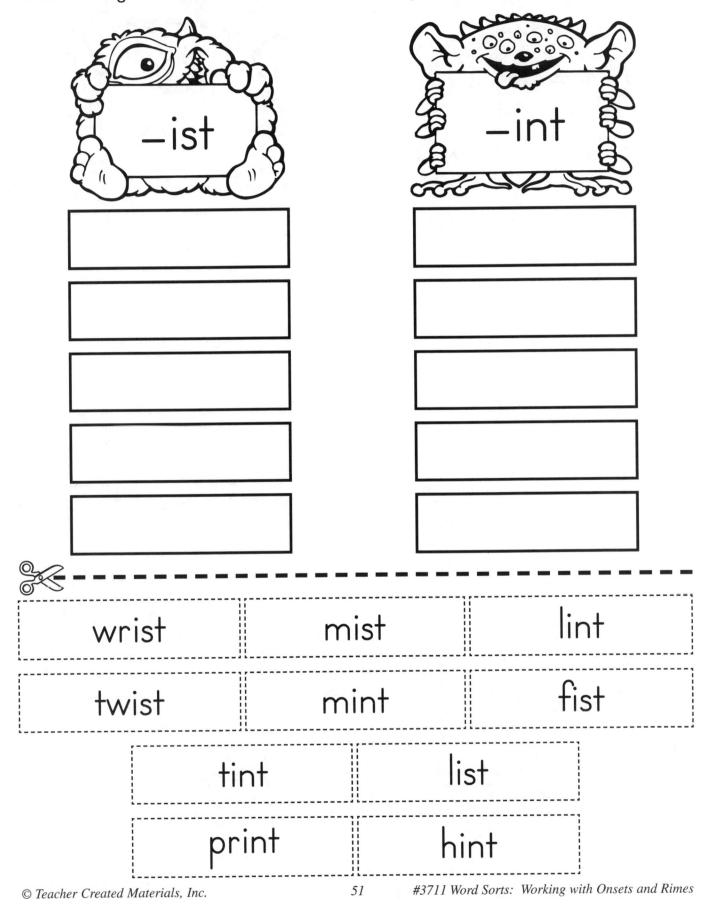

-ist

-int

wrist | mist | lint

twist | mint | fist

tint | list

print | hint

Directions: Cut out the words below. Then sort the words so that all the *–ied* words are together and all the *–ies* words are together.

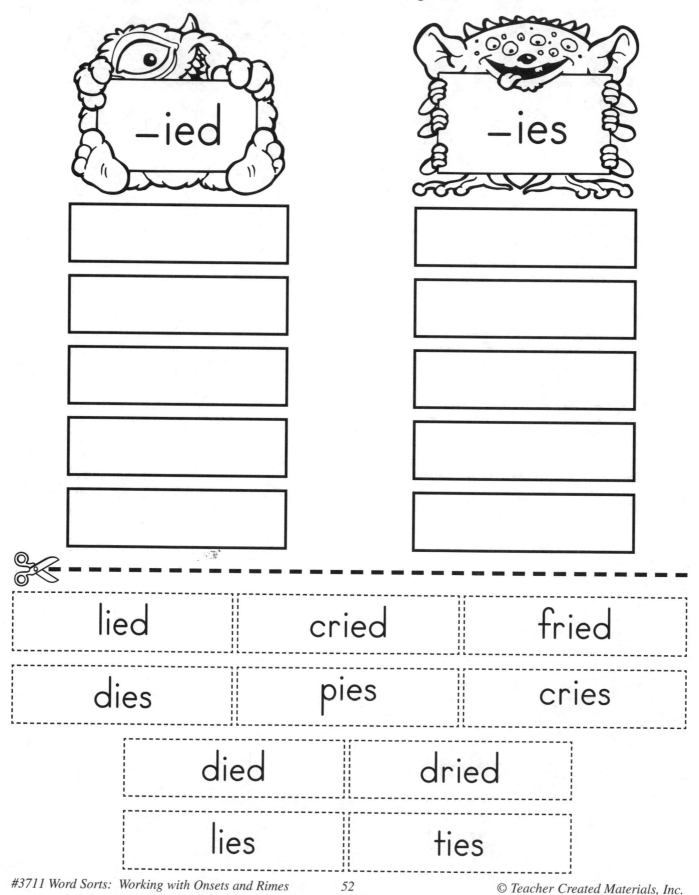

–ied

–ies

| lied | cried | fried |
| dies | pies | cries |

| died | dried |
| lies | ties |

Blend & Single Letter Onsets with Long i Rimes

Directions: Cut out the words below. Then sort the words so that all the *–ife* words are together and all the *–ime* words are together.

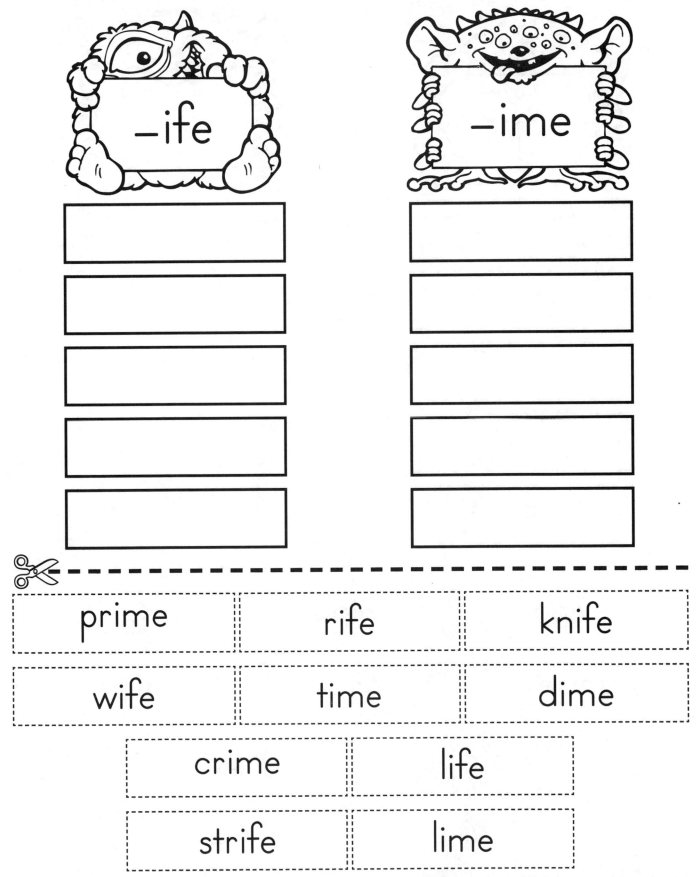

-ife

-ime

prime	rife	knife
wife	time	dime

crime	life
strife	lime

Directions: Cut out the words below. Then sort the words so that all the *–ipe* words are together and all the *–ire* words are together.

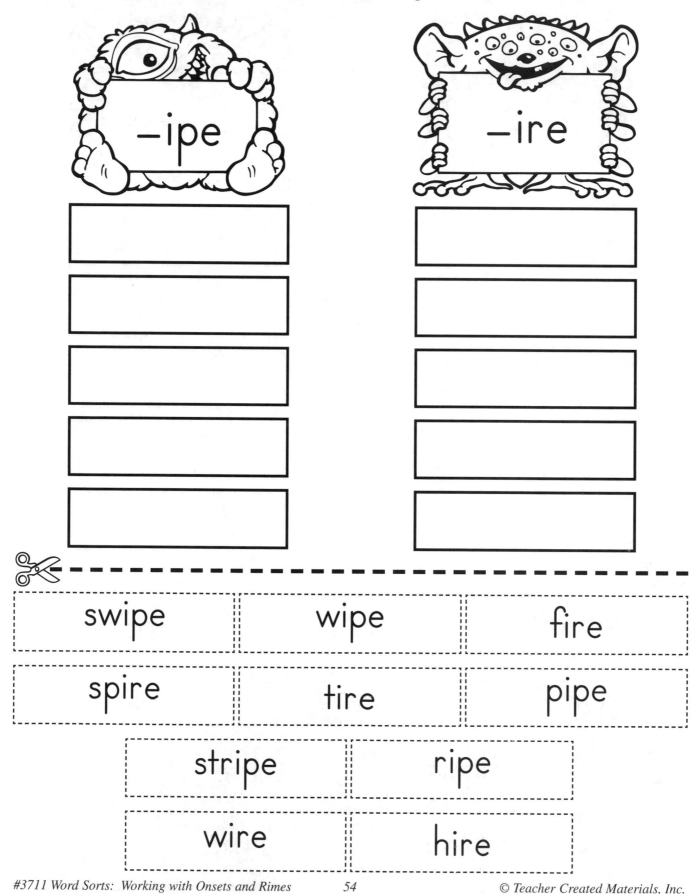

–ipe

–ire

| swipe | wipe | fire |
| spire | tire | pipe |

| stripe | ripe |
| wire | hire |

Blend & Single Letter Onsets with Long o Rimes

Directions: Cut out the words below. Then sort the words so that all the *–oat* words are together and all the *–oke* words are together.

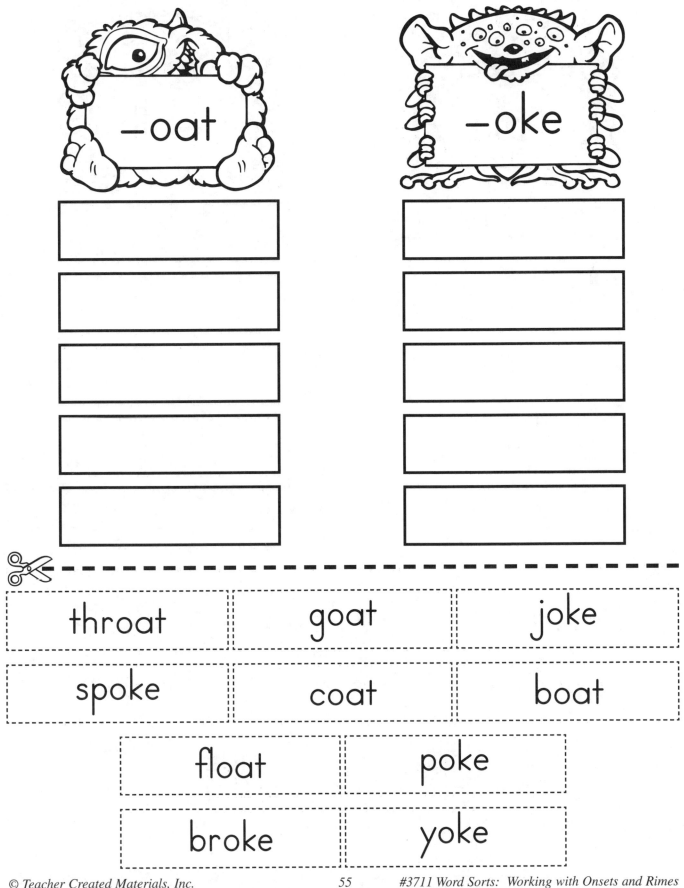

-oat

-oke

✂ -

| throat | goat | joke |
| spoke | coat | boat |

| float | poke |
| broke | yoke |

Directions: Cut out the words below. Then sort the words so that all the *–ole* words are together and all the *–oll* words are together.

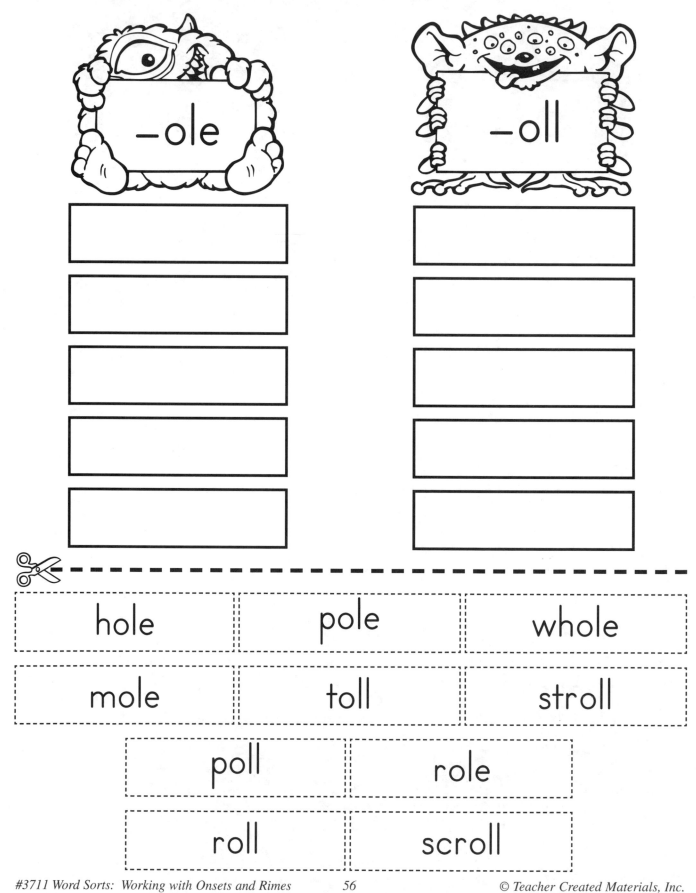

–ole

–oll

hole	pole	whole
mole	toll	stroll

poll	role
roll	scroll

Directions: Cut out the words below. Then sort the words so that all the *–ose* words are together and all the *–ote* words are together.

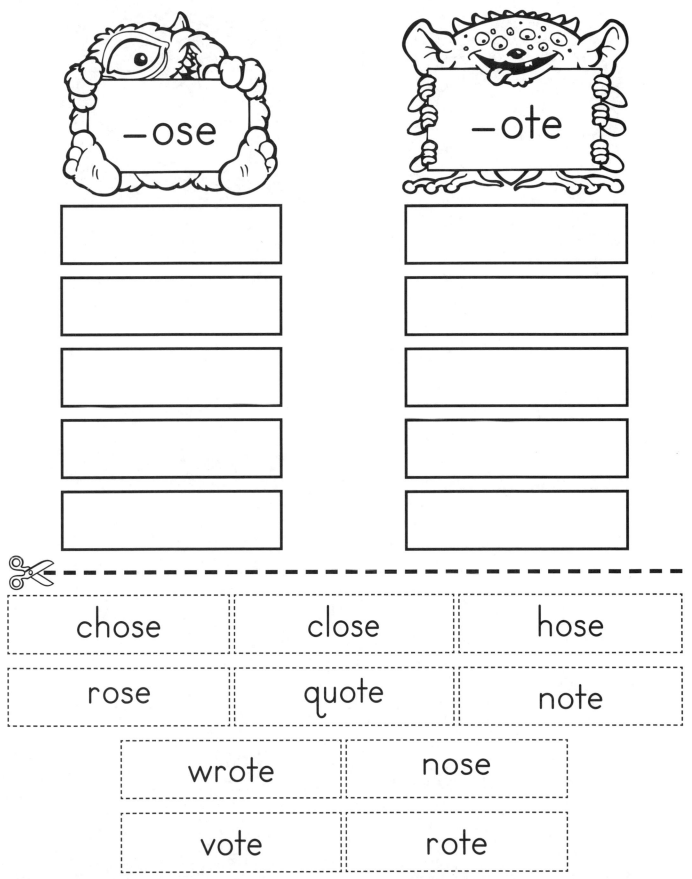

–ose

–ote

chose	close	hose

rose	quote	note

wrote	nose

vote	rote

Blend & Single Letter Onsets with Short u Rimes

Directions: Cut out the words below. Then sort the words so that all the *-ub* words are together and all the *-uck* words are together.

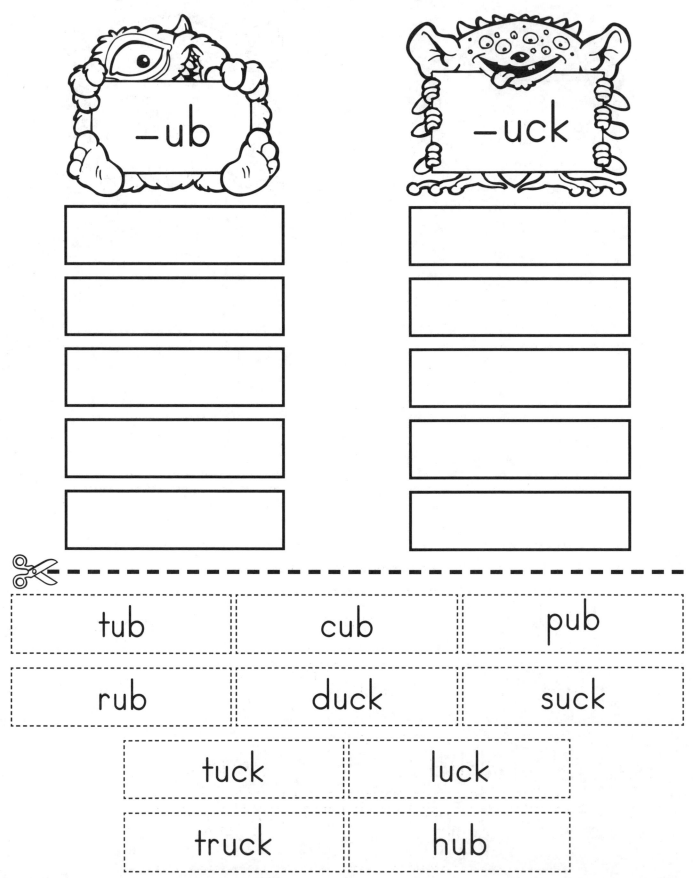

–ub

–uck

tub	cub	pub

rub	duck	suck

tuck	luck

truck	hub

Blend & Single Letter Onsets with Short u Rimes

Directions: Cut out the words below. Then sort the words so that all the *–ud* words are together and all the *–uff* words are together.

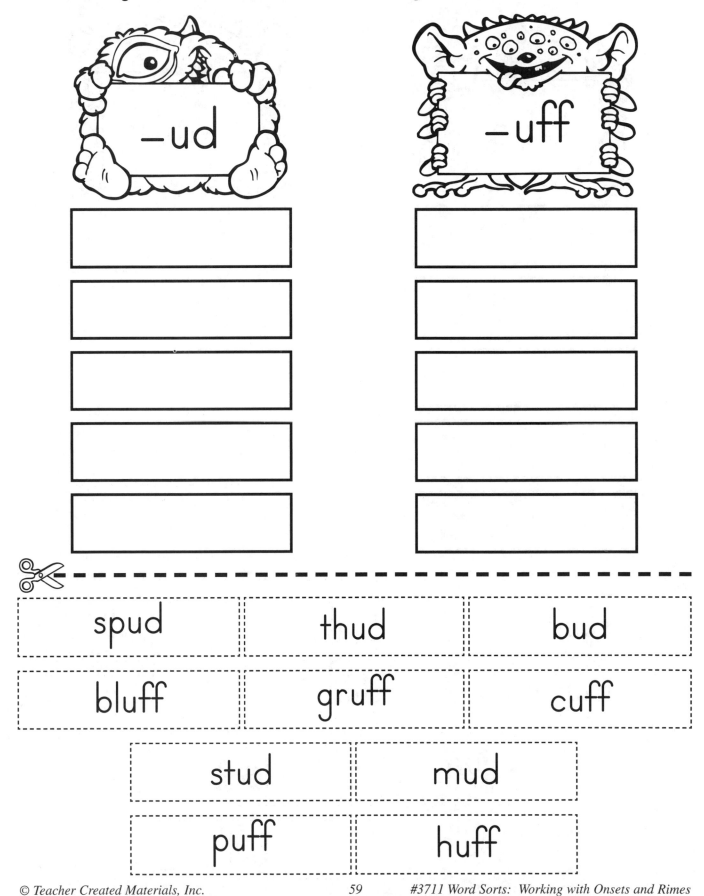

-ud

-uff

spud	thud	bud
bluff	gruff	cuff

stud	mud
puff	huff

Directions: Cut out the words below. Then sort the words so that all the *–ug* words are together and all the *–ull* words are together.

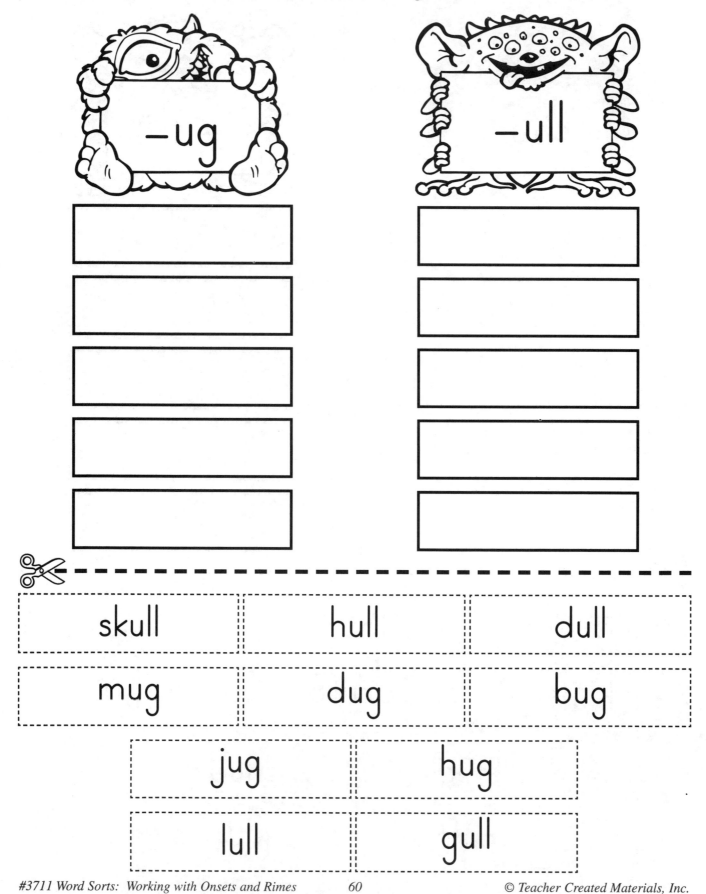

-ug

-ull

skull	hull	dull

mug	dug	bug

jug	hug

lull	gull

Blend & Single Letter Onsets with Short u Rimes

Directions: Cut out the words below. Then sort the words so that all the *–um* words are together and all the *–ump* words are together.

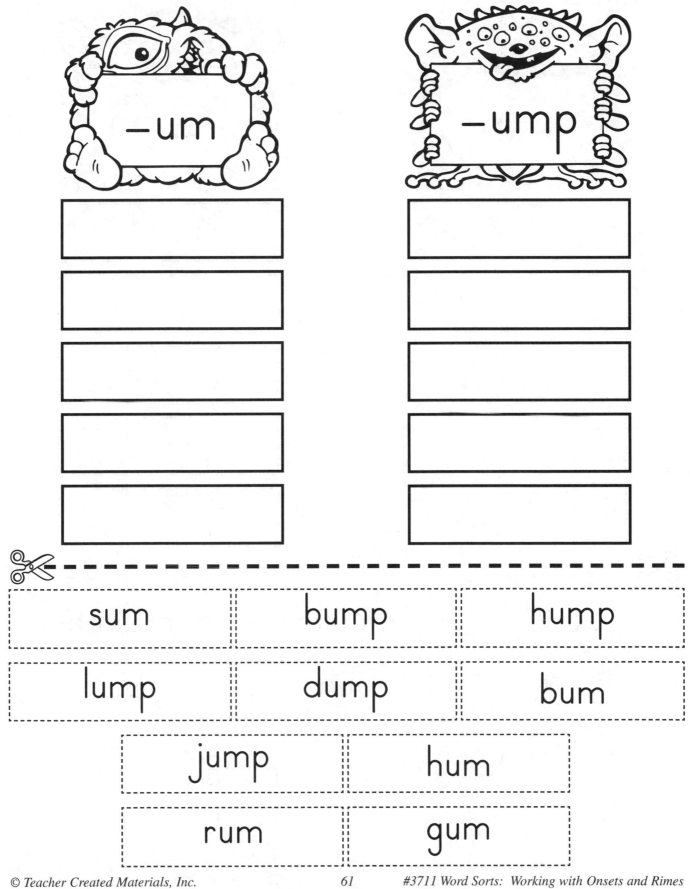

–um

–ump

✂ -

sum	bump	hump
lump	dump	bum

jump	hum
rum	gum

Directions: Cut out the words below. Then sort the words so that all the *–un* words are together and all the *–unch* words are together.

-un

-unch

bun   munch   crunch

lunch   gun   sun

hunch   punch

fun   run

Directions: Cut out the words below. Then sort the words so that all the *–ung* words are together and all the *–unk* words are together.

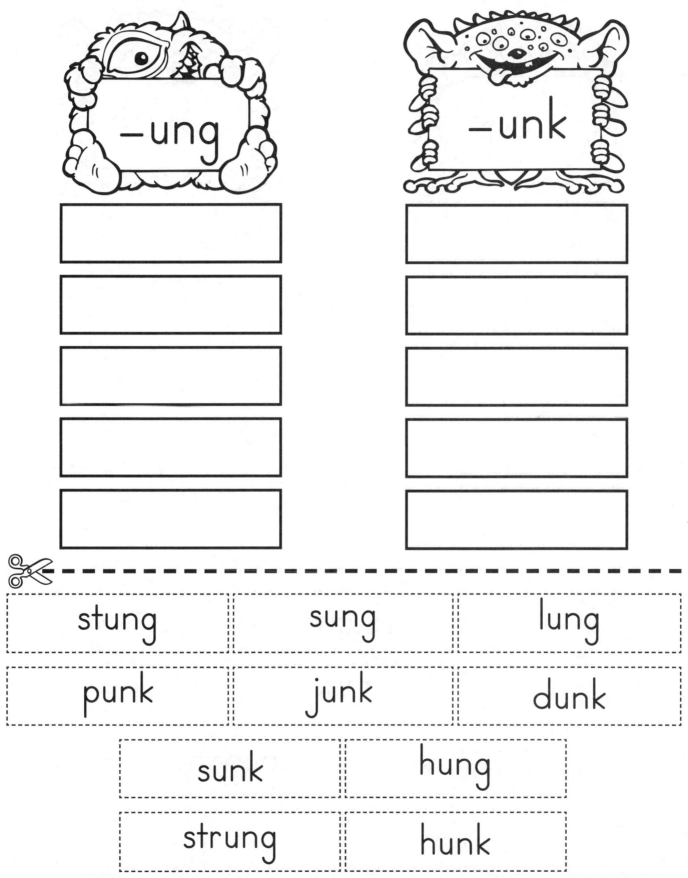

–ung

–unk

| stung | sung | lung |

| punk | junk | dunk |

| sunk | hung |

| strung | hunk |

Directions: Cut out the words below. Then sort the words so that all the *–unt* words are together and all the *–ush* words are together.

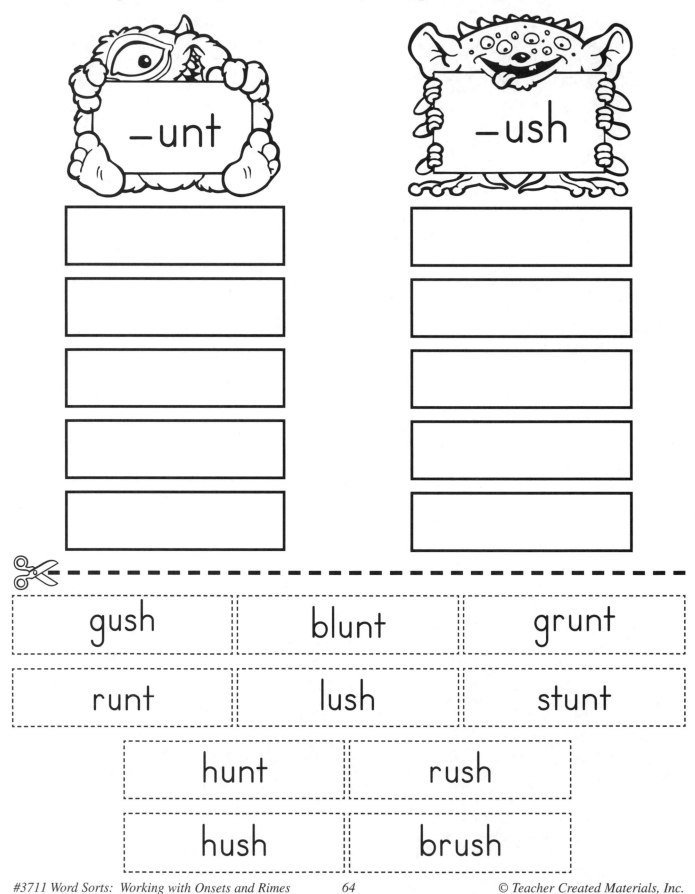

–unt

–ush

gush	blunt	grunt

runt	lush	stunt

hunt	rush
hush	brush

Directions: Cut out the words below. Then sort the words so that all the *–ust* words are together and all the *–ut* words are together.

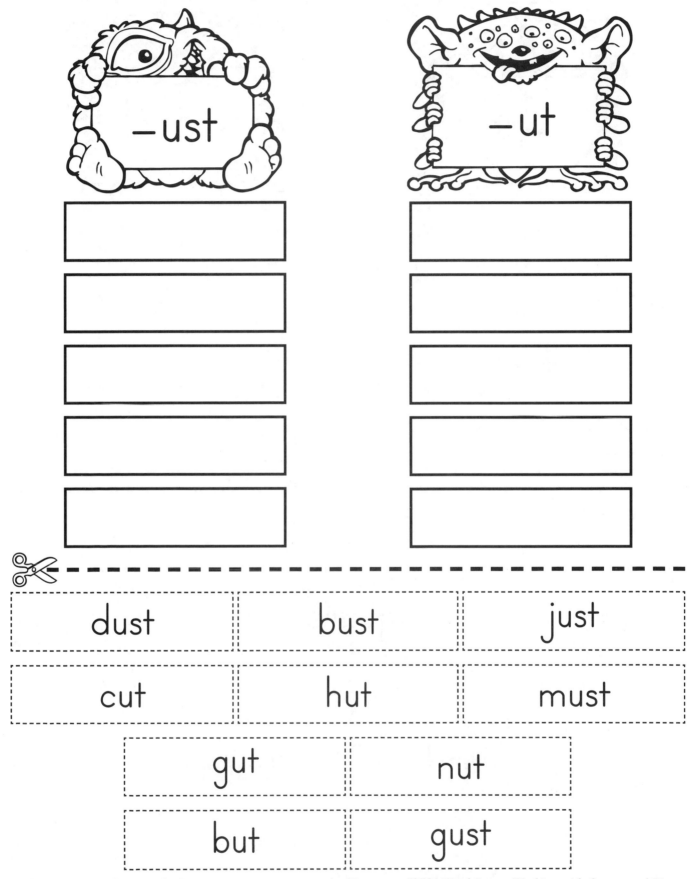

-ust

-ut

| dust | bust | just |
| cut | hut | must |

| gut | nut |

| but | gust |

Directions: Cut out the words below. Then sort the words so that all the *–ar* words are together and all the *–ard* words are together.

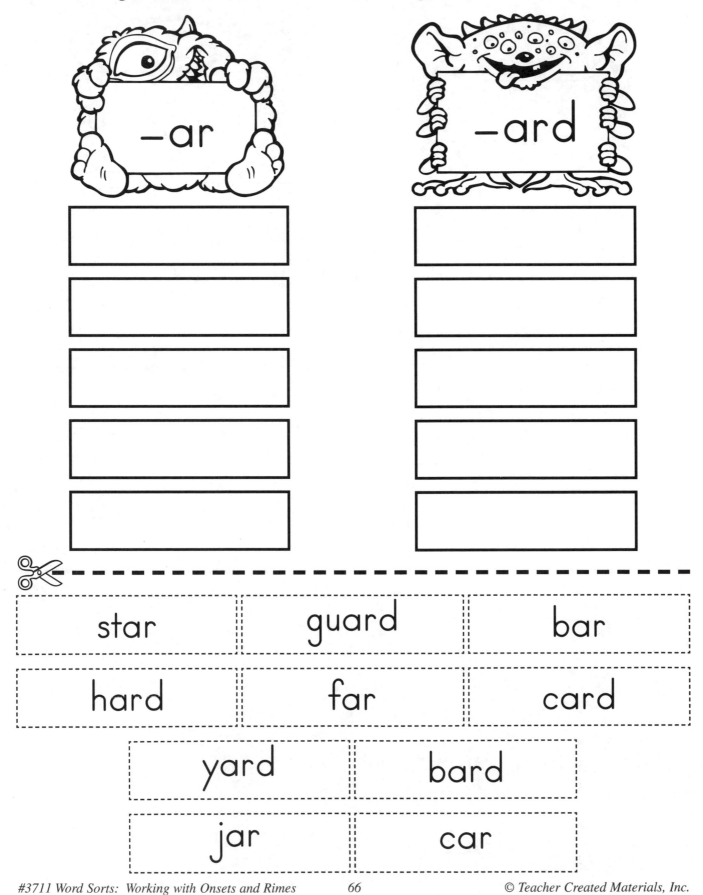

-ar

-ard

| star | guard | bar |

| hard | far | card |

| yard | bard |

| jar | car |

Blend & Single Letter Onsets with Broad a Rimes

Directions: Cut out the words below. Then sort the words so that all the *–ark* words are together and all the *–art* words are together.

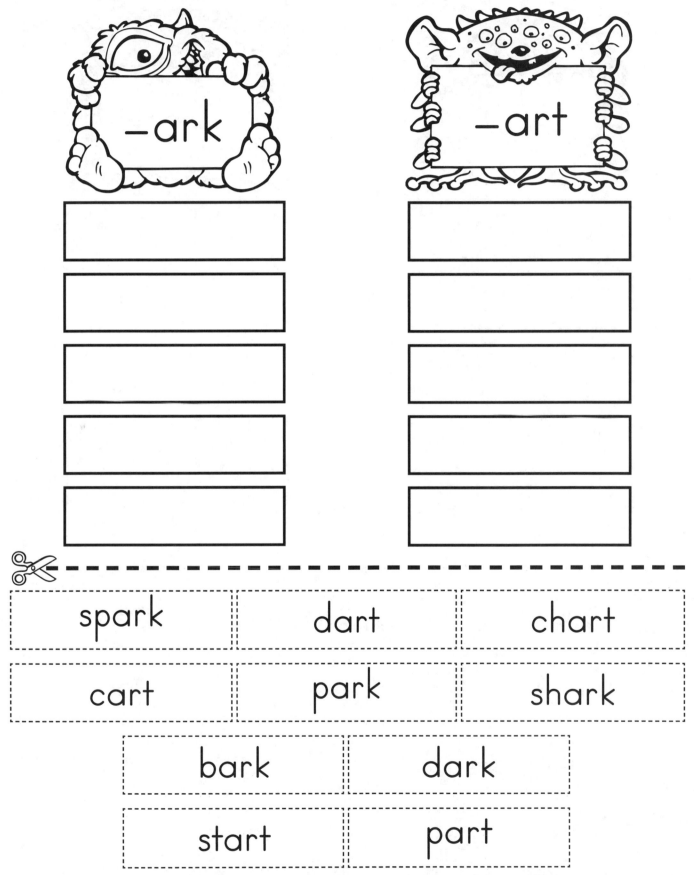

-ark

-art

✂ -

spark	dart	chart
cart	park	shark

bark	dark
start	part

Blend & Single Letter Onsets with Long oo Rimes

Directions: Cut out the words below. Then sort the words so that all the *–ew* words are together and all the *–oo* words are together.

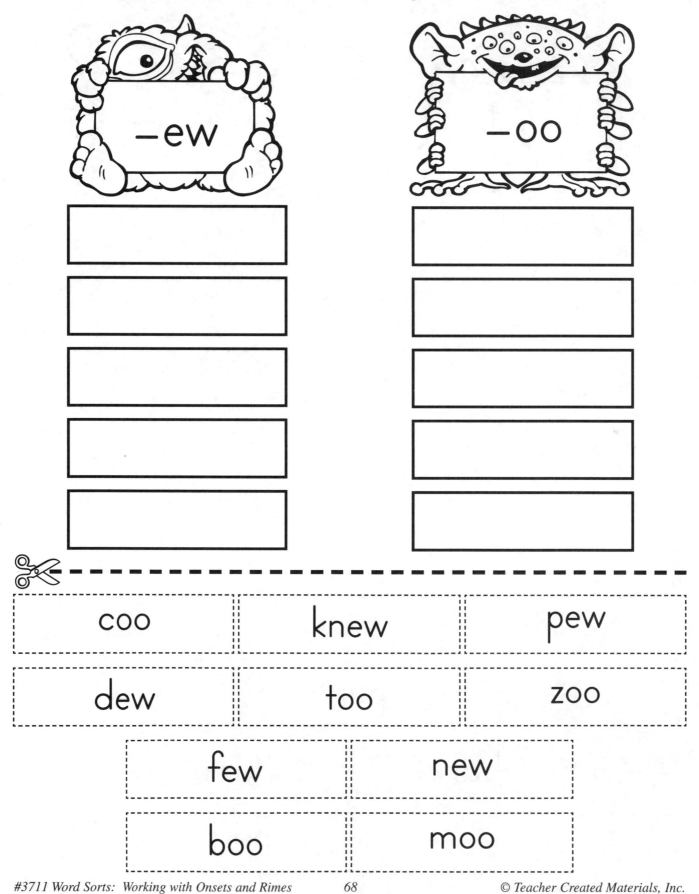

-ew

-oo

coo	knew	pew
dew	too	zoo

few	new
boo	moo

Directions: Cut out the words below. Then sort the words so that all the *–ool* words are together and all the *–oom* words are together.

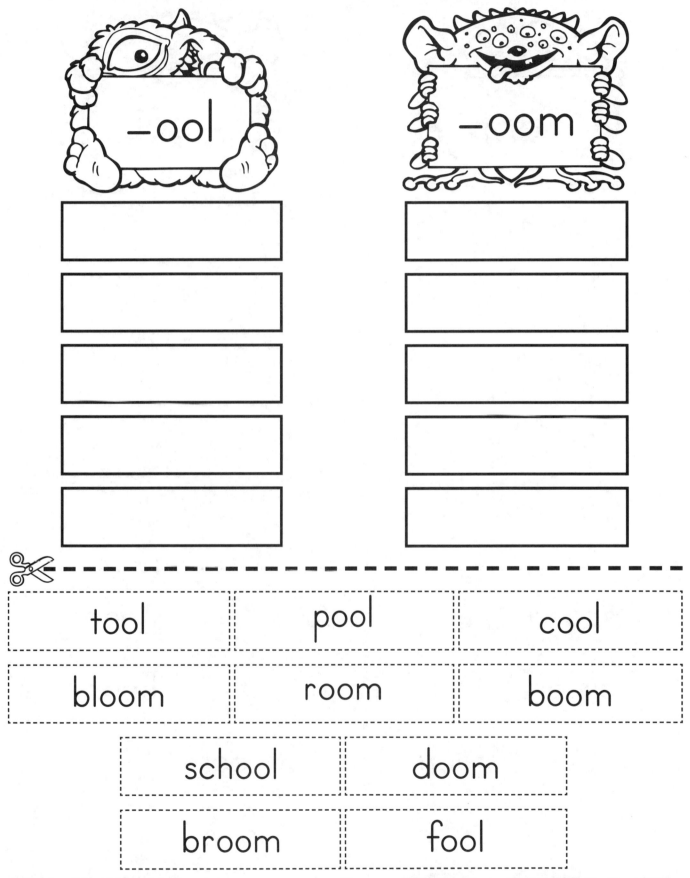

–ool

–oom

tool	pool	cool
bloom	room	boom
school	doom
broom	fool

Directions: Cut out the words below. Then sort the words so that all the *–oon* words are together and all the *–oop* words are together.

–oon

–oop

scoop	troop	noon

croon	soon	hoop

stoop	moon

spoon	loop

Blend & Single Letter Onsets with Long oo Rimes

Directions: Cut out the words below. Then sort the words so that all the *–oot* words are together and all the *–ue* words are together.

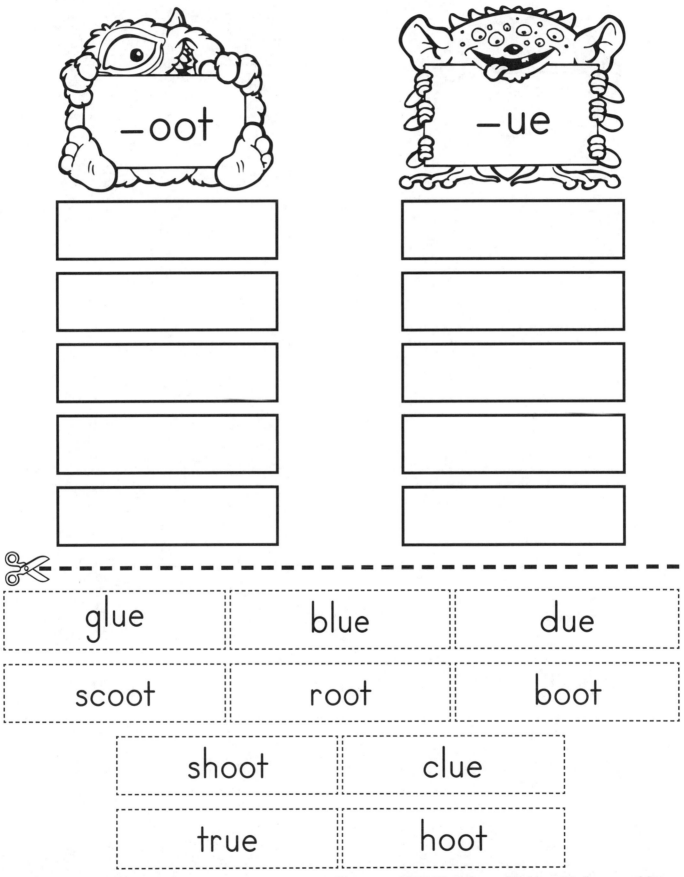

| glue | blue | due |
| scoot | root | boot |

| shoot | clue |
| true | hoot |

Blend & Single Letter Onsets with Broad o Rimes

Directions: Cut out the words below. Then sort the words so that all the *–all* words are together and all the *–alk* words are together.

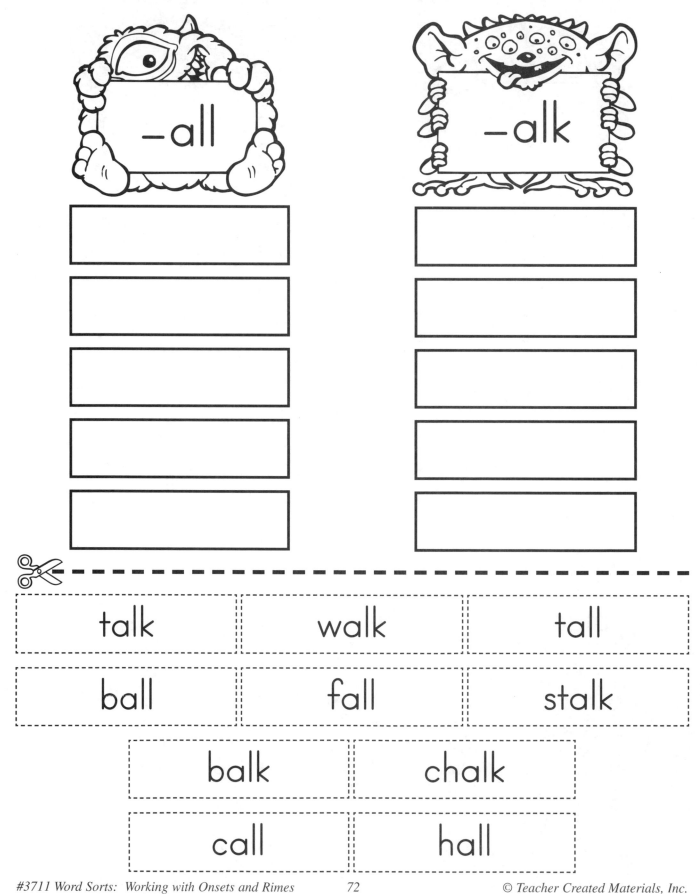

–all

–alk

talk	walk	tall
ball	fall	stalk

balk	chalk
call	hall

Directions: Cut out the words below. Then sort the words so that all the *–aw* words are together and all the *–awl* words are together.

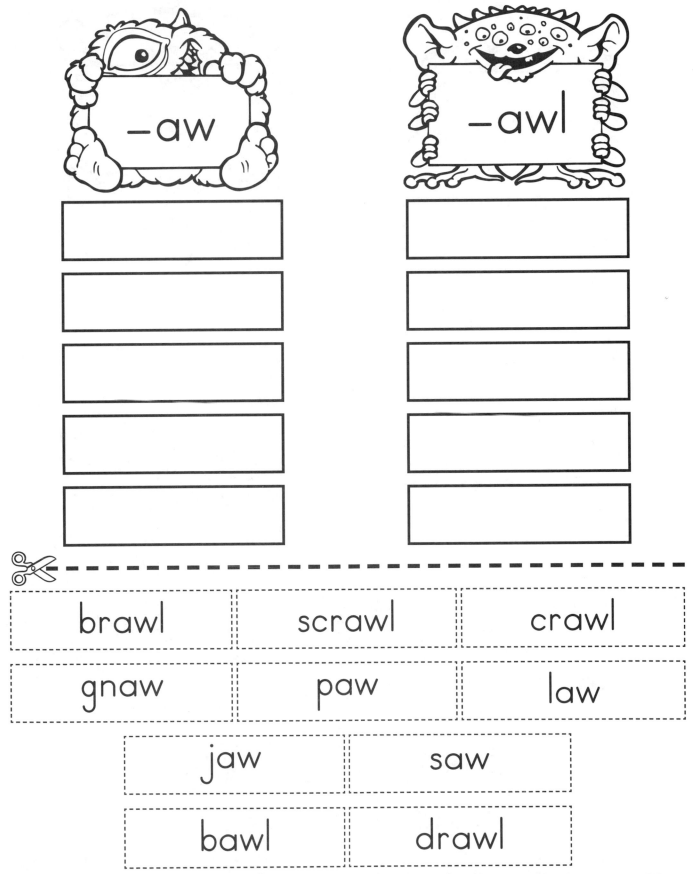

-aw

-awl

| brawl | scrawl | crawl |
| gnaw | paw | law |

| jaw | saw |
| bawl | drawl |

Blend & Single Letter Onsets with Broad o Rimes

Directions: Cut out the words below. Then sort the words so that all the *–awn* words are together and all the *–ong* words are together.

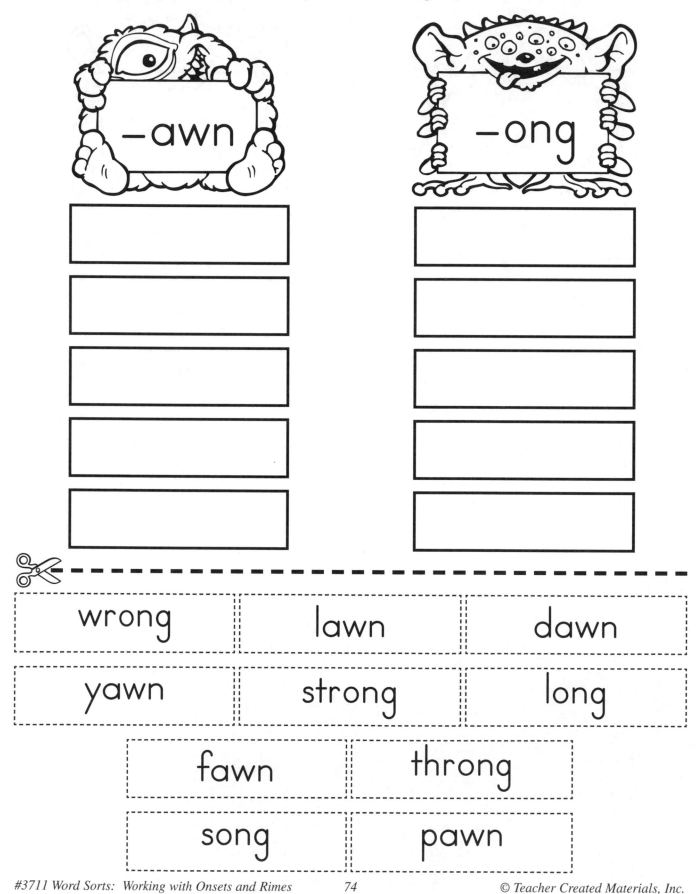

-awn

-ong

wrong	lawn
dawn	
yawn	strong
long	
fawn	throng
song	pawn

Blend & Single Letter Onsets with Broad o Rimes

Directions: Cut out the words below. Then sort the words so that all the *–ore* words are together and all the *–ord* words are together.

-ore

-ord

cord	sore	lord

core	wore	more

bore	chord

ford	sword

Directions: Cut out the words below. Then sort the words so that all the *–orn* words are together and all the *–ort* words are together.

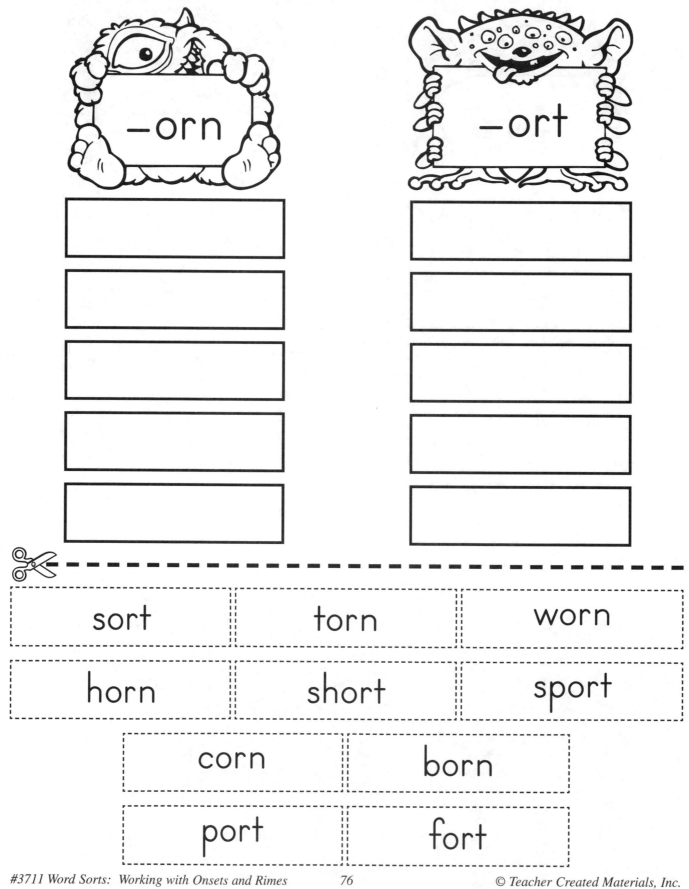

–orn

–ort

sort	torn	worn

horn	short	sport

corn	born

port	fort

Directions: Cut out the words below. Then sort the words so that all the *–oss* words are together and all the *–oth* words are together.

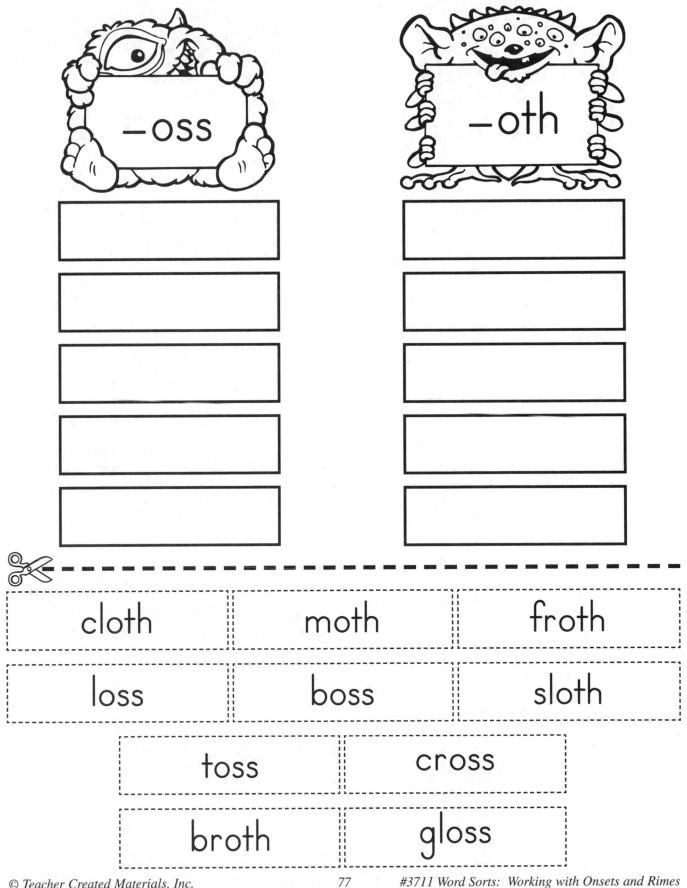

–oss

–oth

cloth   moth   froth

loss   boss   sloth

toss   cross

broth   gloss

Directions: Cut out the words below. Then sort the words so that all the *–ound* words are together and all the *–out* words are together.

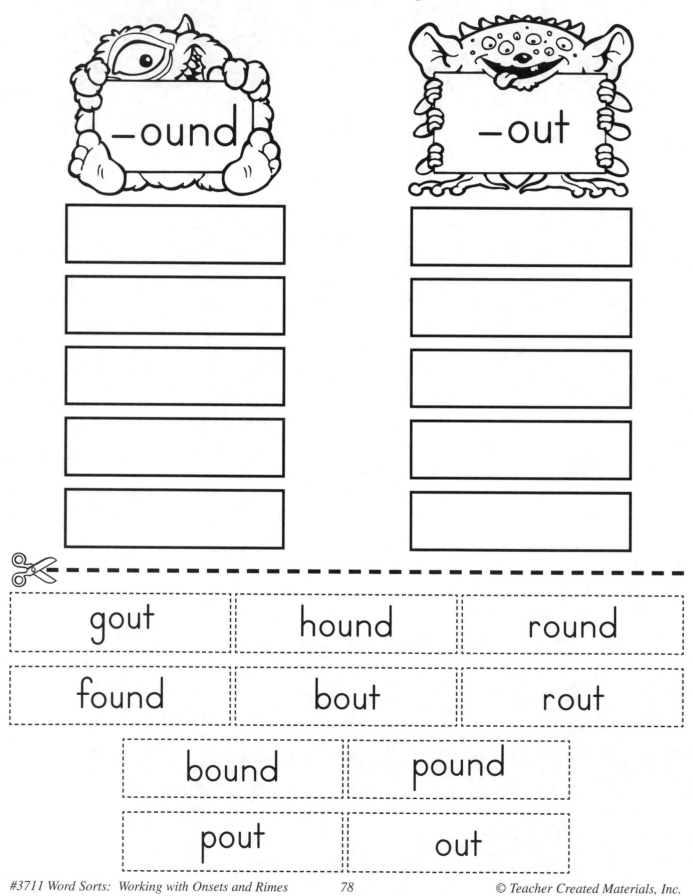

–ound

–out

gout	hound	round
found	bout	rout

bound	pound

pout	out

Directions: Cut out the words below. Then sort the words so that all the *–ow* words are together and all the *–own* words are together.

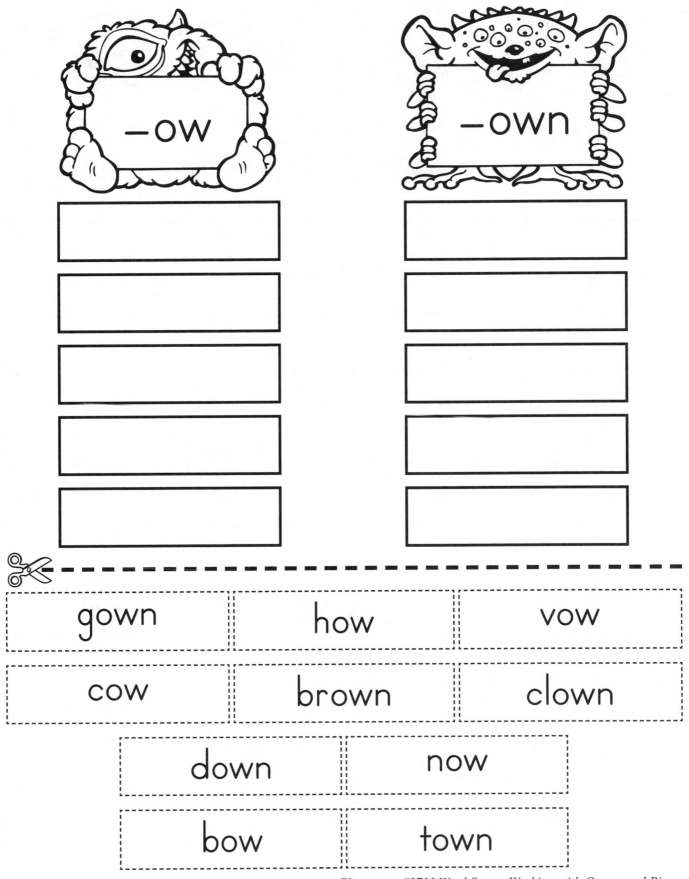

–ow

–own

gown	how	vow
cow	brown	clown
down	now	
bow	town	

Triple Sorts with Less Common Rimes

Directions: Cut out the words below. Then sort the words so that all the *–ask* words are together, all the *–asp* words are together, and all the *–ax* words are together.

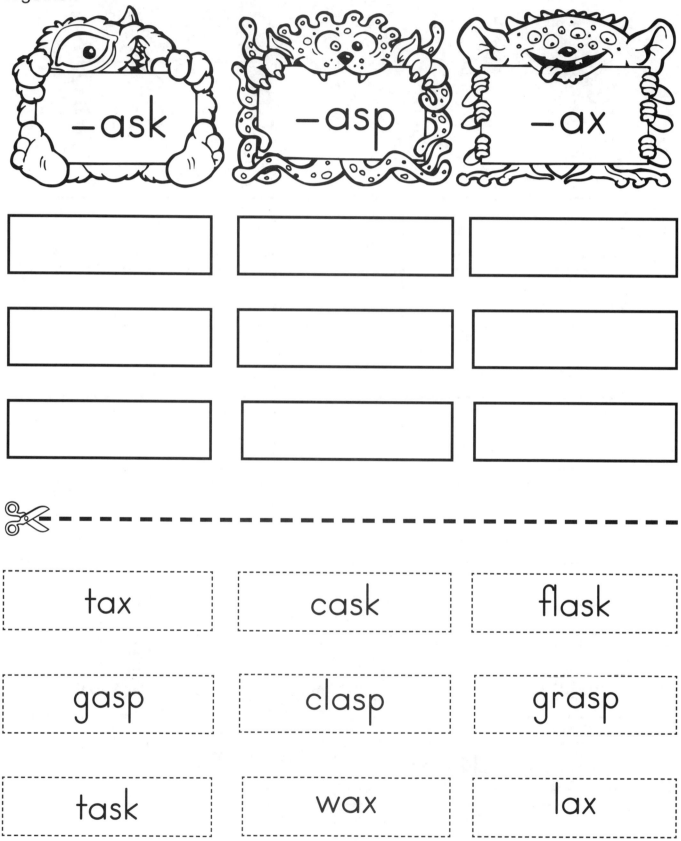

-ask   -asp   -ax

tax	cask	flask
gasp	clasp	grasp
task	wax	lax

Triple Sorts with Less Common Rimes

Directions: Cut out the words below. Then sort the words so that all the *–age* words are together, all the *–aid* words are together, and all the *–ait* words are together.

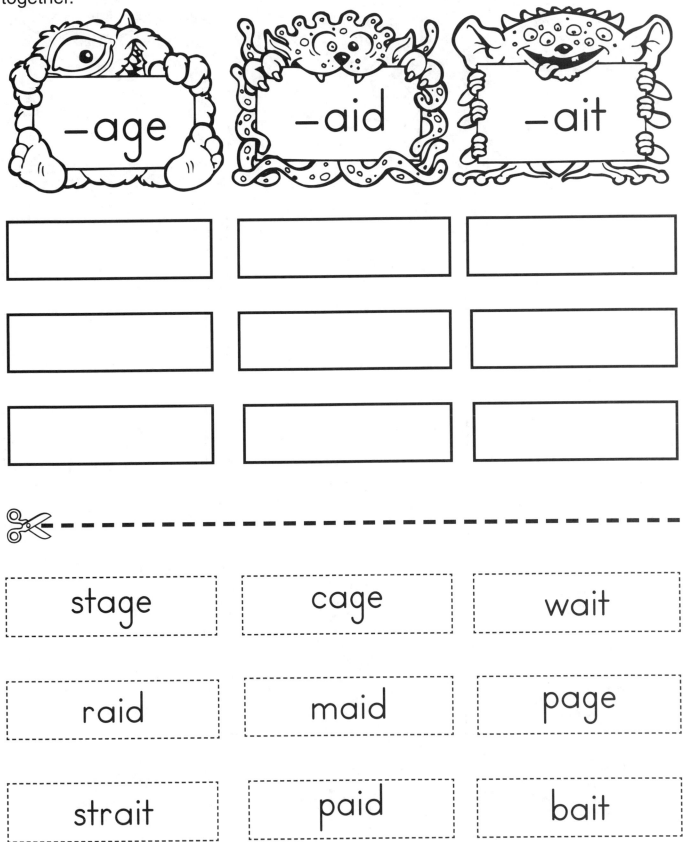

-age   -aid   -ait

stage	cage	wait
raid	maid	page
strait	paid	bait

Directions: Cut out the words below. Then sort the words so that all the *–ase* words are together, all the *–aste* words are together, and all the *–aint* words are together.

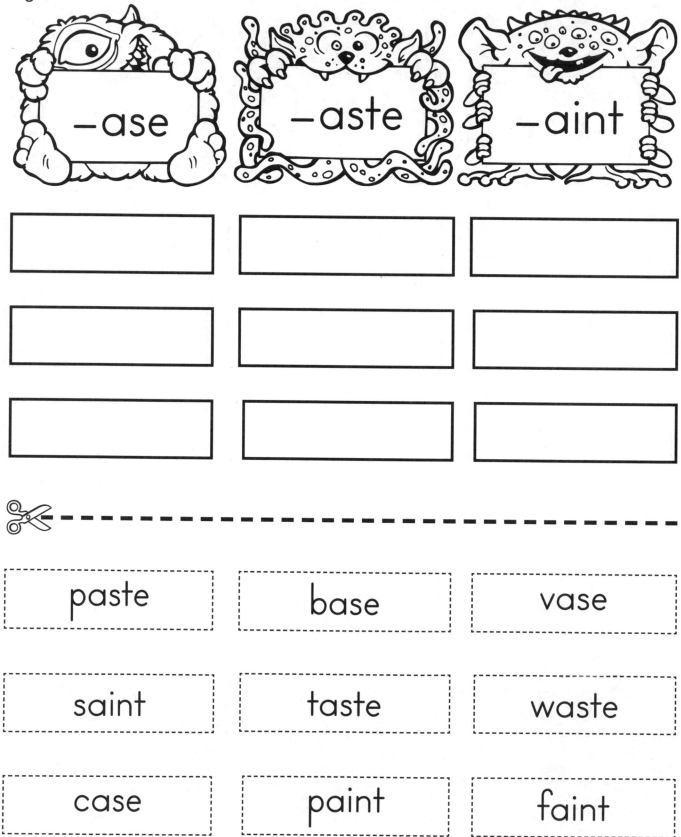

Triple Sorts with Less Common Rimes

Directions: Cut out the words below. Then sort the words so that all the *–arm* words are together, all the *–arn* words are together, and all the *–arp* words are together.

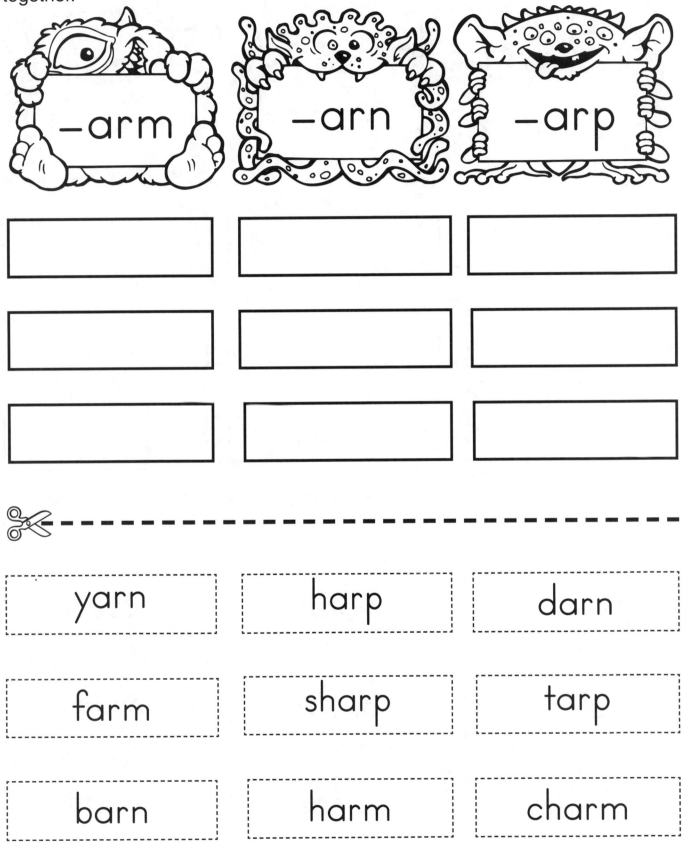

-arm

-arn

-arp

yarn

harp

darn

farm

sharp

tarp

barn

harm

charm

Triple Sorts with Less Common Rimes

Directions: Cut out the words below. Then sort the words so that all the *–ead* words are together, all the *–ear* words are together, and all the *–ealth* words are together.

-ead   -ear   -ealth

wealth   health   dead

bear   bread   swear

head   wear   stealth

Directions: Cut out the words below. Then sort the words so that all the *–edge* words are together, all the *–eft* words are together, and all the *–eg* words are together.

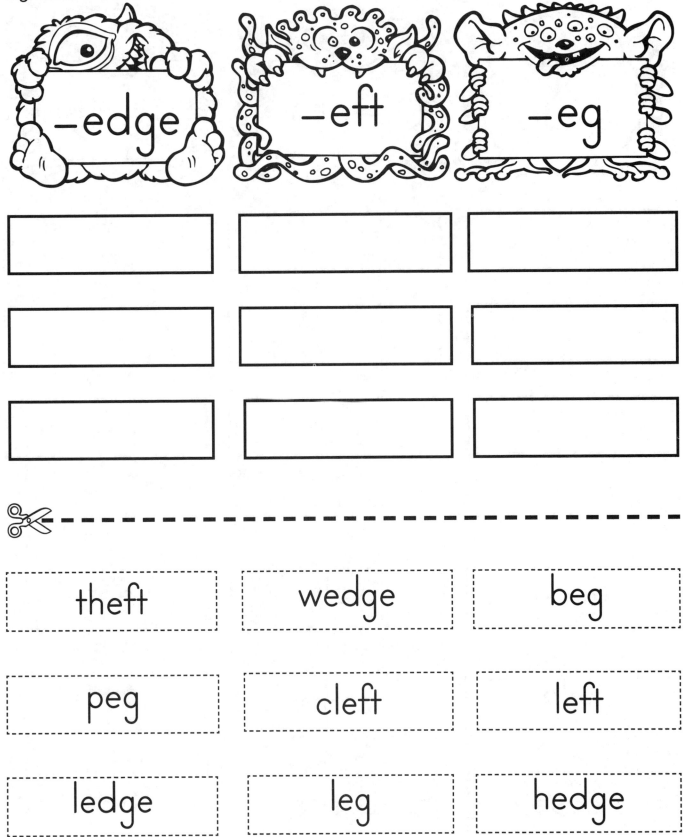

-edge   -eft   -eg

theft   wedge   beg

peg   cleft   left

ledge   leg   hedge

Directions: Cut out the words below. Then sort the words so that all the *–elp* words are together, all the *–em* words are together, and all the *–ense* words are together.

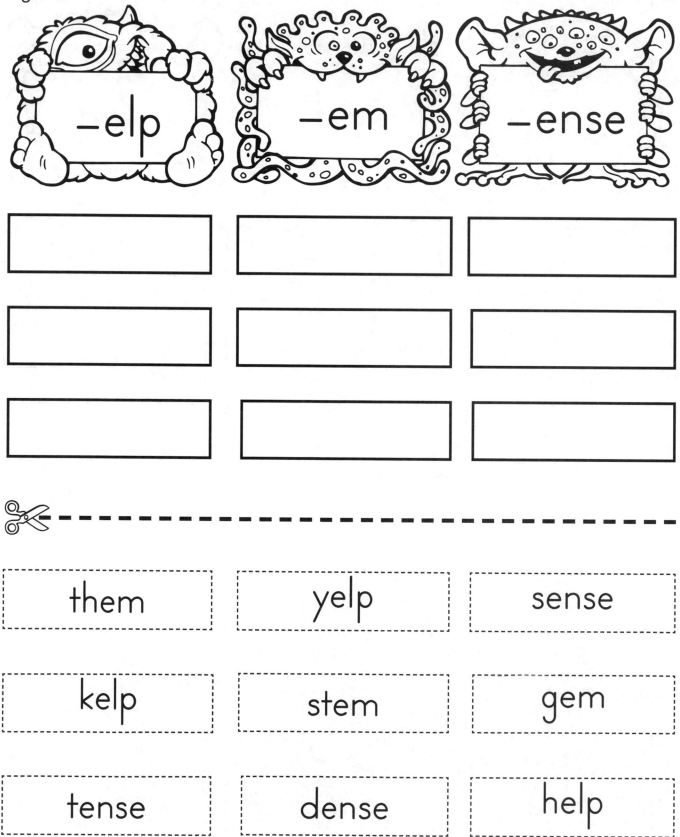

–elp

–em

–ense

them	yelp	sense
kelp	stem	gem
tense	dense	help

Triple Sorts with Less Common Rimes

Directions: Cut out the words below. Then sort the words so that all the *–ep* words are together, all the *–esh* words are together, and all the *–ex* words are together.

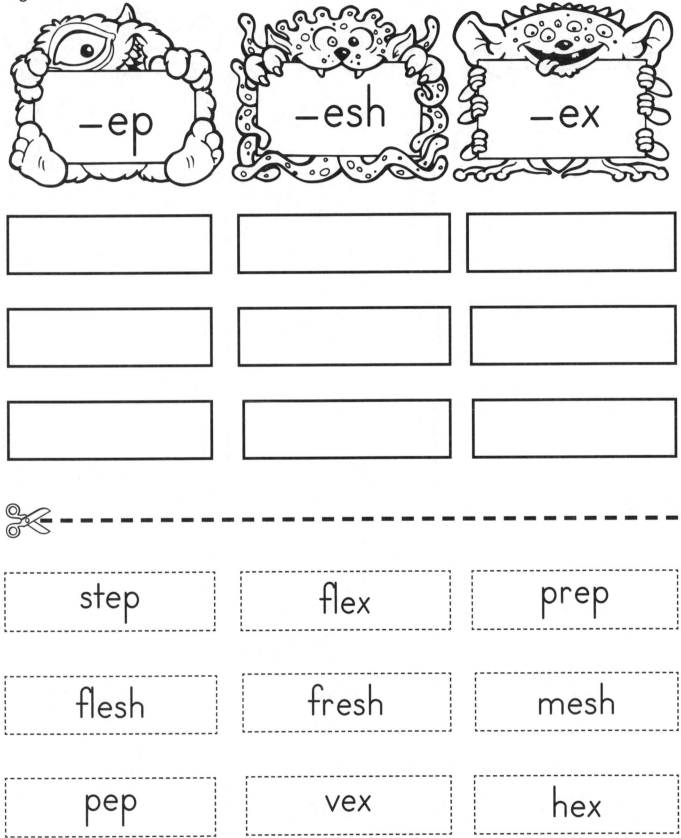

-ep   -esh   -ex

step   flex   prep

flesh   fresh   mesh

pep   vex   hex

Directions: Cut out the words below. Then sort the words so that all the *-e* words are together, all the *-ea* words are together, and all the *-ead* words are together.

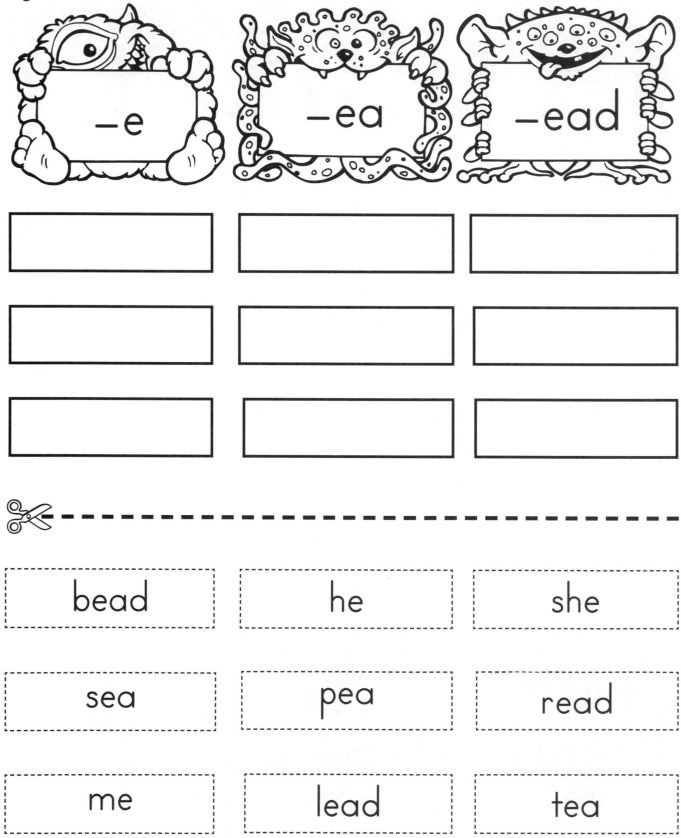

-e   -ea   -ead

bead	he	she
sea	pea	read
me	lead	tea

Triple Sorts with Less Common Rimes

Directions: Cut out the words below. Then sort the words so that all the *–eap* words are together, all the *–ease* words are together, and all the *–east* words are together.

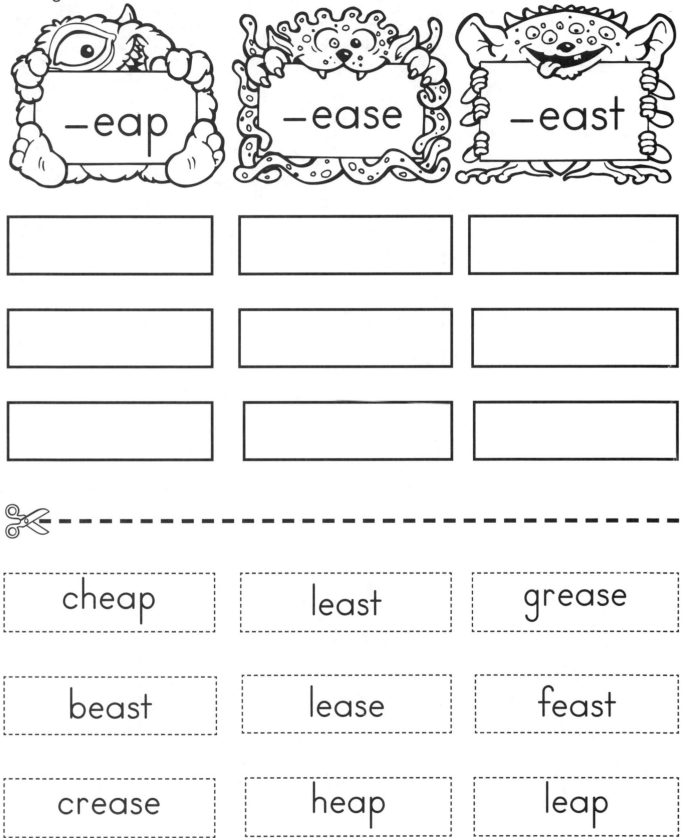

-eap   -ease   -east

cheap   least   grease

beast   lease   feast

crease   heap   leap

Directions: Cut out the words below. Then sort the words so that all the *–eech* words are together, all the *–ief* words are together, and all the *–ield* words are together.

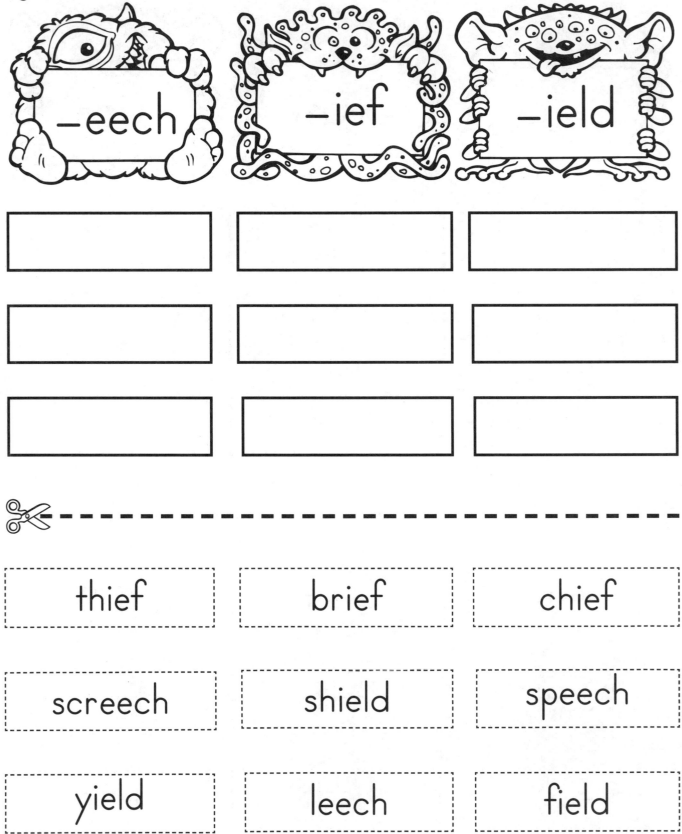

-eech   -ief   -ield

thief   brief   chief

screech   shield   speech

yield   leech   field

Triple Sorts with Less Common Rimes

Directions: Cut out the words below. Then sort the words so that all the *–ilk* words are together, all the *–in* words are together, and all the *–ish* words are together.

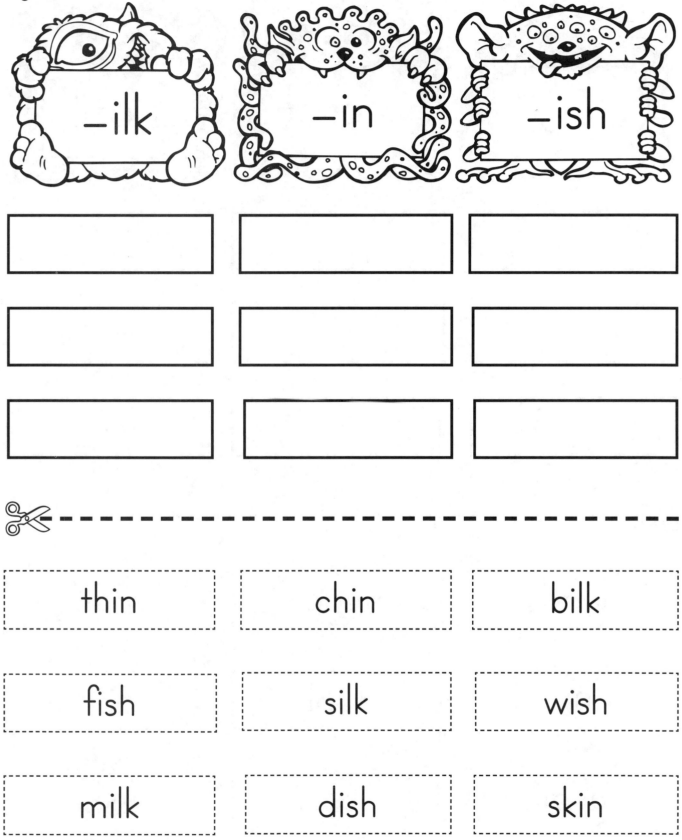

–ilk   –in   –ish

thin	chin	bilk
fish	silk	wish
milk	dish	skin

© Teacher Created Materials, Inc.   91   *#3711 Word Sorts: Working with Onsets and Rimes*

Triple Sorts with Less Common Rimes

Directions: Cut out the words below. Then sort the words so that all the *–o* words are together, all the *–oad* words are together, and all the *–oal* words are together.

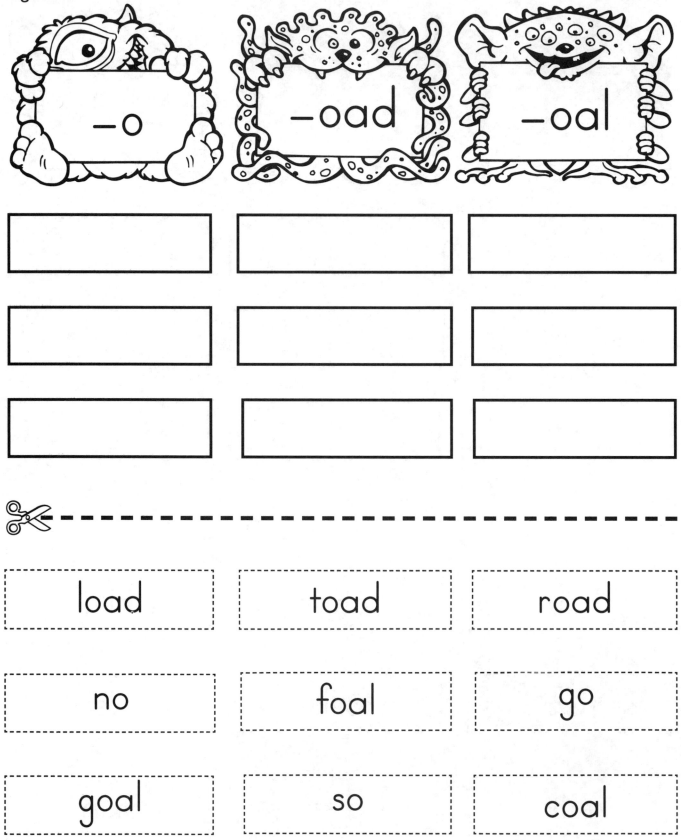

-o

-oad

-oal

✂ --

| load | toad | road |

| no | foal | go |

| goal | so | coal |

Directions: Cut out the words below. Then sort the words so that all the *–oast* words are together, all the *–oe* words are together, and all the *–ost* words are together.

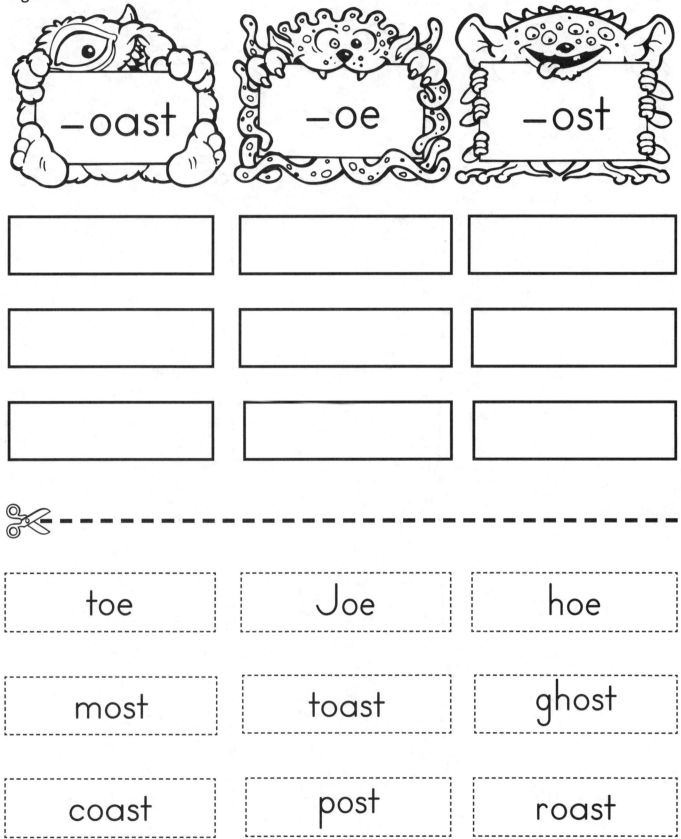

-oast   -oe   -ost

toe	Joe	hoe
most	toast	ghost
coast	post	roast

Triple Sorts with Less Common Rimes

Directions: Cut out the words below. Then sort the words so that all the *–ood* words are together, all the *–ook* words are together, and all the *–ould* words are together.

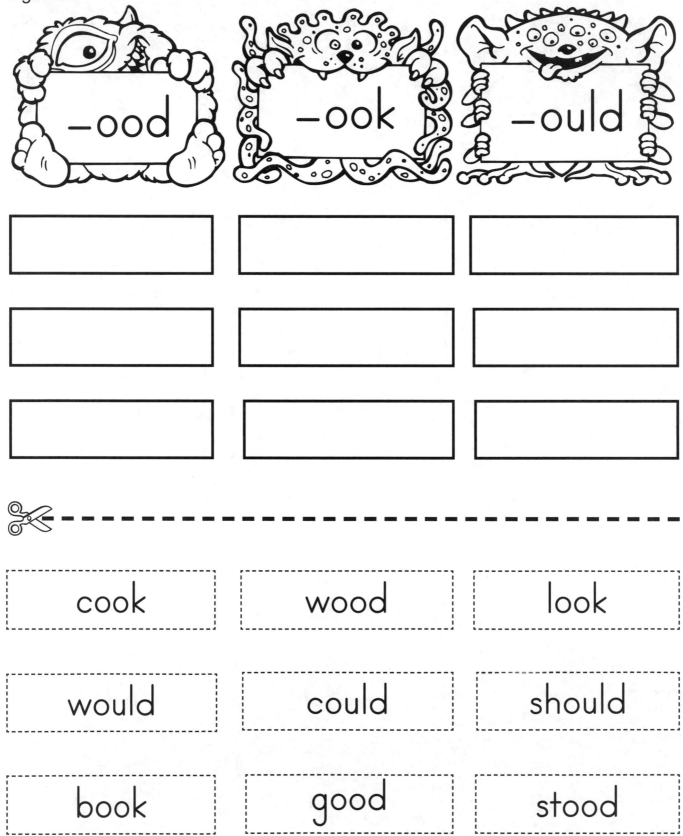

–ood   –ook   –ould

cook	wood	look
would	could	should
book	good	stood

Page 4
–ad: had, lad, sad, mad, bad
–ag: bag, rag, sag, wag, nag

Page 5
–ab: cab, jab, lab, nab, tab
–ack: back, lack, pack, sack, tack

Page 6
–am: dam, ham, jam, ram, yam
–amp: camp, damp, lamp, ramp, vamp

Page 7
–an: ban, can, fan, man, pan
–and: band, hand, land, sand, stand

Page 8
–ap: cap, gap, lap, map, nap
–at: bat, cat, fat, hat, sat

Page 9
–ace: face, lace, mace, pace, race
–ail: bail, fail, hail, jail, mail

Page 10
–ake: bake, cake, fake, lake, make
–ale: bale, hale, male, sale, tale

Page 11
–ame: came, fame, game, name, same
–ane: cane, lane, mane, pane, sane

Page 12
–ate: date, fate, gate, hate, late
–ave: cave, gave, pave, save, wave

Page 13
–ay: bay, day, hay, lay, may
–aze: daze, faze, gaze, haze, maze

Page 14
–ed: bed, fed, led, red, wed
–ell: bell, cell, fell, sell, tell

Page 15
–en: den, hen, men, pen, ten
–end: bend, lend, mend, send, tend

Page 16
–ent: bent, cent, dent, lent, tent
–est: best, nest, pest, rest, test

Page 17
–et: bet, get, met, pet, let
–elt: belt, felt, melt, welt, pelt

Page 18
–eak: beak, leak, peak, teak, weak
–eal: deal, heal, meal, real, seal

Page 19
–ear: dear, fear, hear, near, tear
–eat: beat, heat, meat, neat, seat

Page 20
–ee: bee, fee, see, wee, free
–eed: deed, need, feed, weed, seed

Page 21
–eek: leek, meek, peek, seek, week
–eel: feel, heel, kneel, peel, reel

Page 22
–eep: beep, deep, keep, seep, weep
–eer: beer, deer, leer, peer, seer

Page 23
–ick: kick, lick, pick, sick, tick
–id: bid, did, hid, lid, rid

Page 24
–ill: bill, fill, hill, pill, kill
–in: pin, bin, fin, win, sin

Page 25
–ing: wing, sing, ring, king, bring
–ink: sink, pink, mink, link, wink

Page 26
–ip: dip, lip, sip, rip, tip
–it: bit, sit, kit, hit, fit

Page 27
–ice: vice, rice, nice, mice, dice
–ide: wide, tide, side, ride, hide

Page 28
–ie: die, tie, vie, pie, lie
–ight: fight, right, night, light, might

Page 29
–ike: pike, like, hike, dike, bike
–ile: vile, tile, pile, mile, file

Page 30
–ind: find, kind, mind, wind, bind
–ine: mine, nine, fine, line, dine

Page 31
–ob: cob, sob, gob, job, rob
–ock: dock, clock, lock, sock, rock

Page 32
–od: nod, rod, sod, trod, plod
–og: bog, dog, fog, jog, hog

Page 33
–op: top, pop, mop, hop, cop
–ot: pot, not, hot, got, dot

Page 34
–old: bold, fold, cold, gold, sold
–one: lone, cone, bone, zone, tone

Page 35
–ope: rope, pope, nope, hope, cope
–ow: sow, mow, row, low, bow

Page 36
–ance: trance, chance, lance, dance, glance
–ang: rang, sang, gang, bang, hang

Page 37
–ank: bank, rank, lank, sank, tank
–ant: can't, pant, rant, chant, plant

Page 38
–ash: bash, cash, dash, mash, rash
–ast: past, mast, cast, fast, last

Page 39
–atch: batch, catch, hatch, match, patch
–ass: bass, lass, mass, pass, glass

Page 40
–ain: lain, vain, main, rain, pain
–ape: cape, shape, gape, grape, tape

Page 41
–ame: blame, flame, frame, shame, name
–ane: Jane, crane, lane, cane, plane

Page 42
–eck: peck, neck, deck, check, wreck
–elt: knelt, felt, belt, melt, welt

Page 43
–ench: bench, wench, clench, drench, wrench
–ess: guess, mess, less, chess, dress

Page 44
–each: bleach, peach, beach, reach, teach
–eam: beam, seam, cream, dream, team

Page 45
–ean: lean, dean, bean, mean, clean
–eet: beet, feet, meet, greet, sheet

Page 46
–een: green, teen, seen, queen, keen
–eeze: tweeze, squeeze, sneeze, freeze, breeze

Page 47
–ib: bib, glib, fib, crib, rib
–ift: gift, drift, rift, lift, sift

Page 48
–ig: pig, wig, fig, dig, big
–ilt: wilt, tilt, kilt, jilt, hilt

Page 49
–im: dim, rim, him, brim, grim
–inch: cinch, finch, pinch, clinch, winch

Page 50
–isk: whisk, frisk, brisk, risk, disk
–iss: bliss, Swiss, miss, kiss, hiss

Page 51
–ist: wrist, twist, mist, list, fist
–int: tint, print, mint, hint, lint

Page 52
–ied: lied, died, cried, dried, fried
–ies: dies, lies, pies, ties, cries

Page 53
–ife: wife, strife, rife, life, knife
–ime: prime, crime, time, lime, dime

Page 54
–ipe: swipe, stripe, wipe, ripe, pipe
–ire: spire, wire, tire, hire, fire

Page 55
–oat: throat, float, goat, coat, boat
–oke: spoke, broke, poke, yoke, joke

Page 56
–ole: hole, mole, pole, role, whole
–oll: poll, roll, toll, scroll, stroll

Page 57
–ose: chose, rose, close, nose, hose
–ote: wrote, vote, quote, rote, note

Page 58
–ub: tub, rub, cub, hub, pub
–uck: tuck, truck, duck, luck, suck

Page 59
–ud: spud, stud, thud, mud, bud
–uff: bluff, puff, gruff, huff, cuff

Page 60
–ug: mug, jug, dug, hug, bug
–ull: skull, lull, hull, gull, dull

Page 61
–um: sum, rum, hum, gum, bum
–ump: lump, jump, bump, dump, hump

Page 62
–un: bun, fun, gun, run, sun
–unch: lunch, hunch, munch, punch, crunch

Page 63
–ung: stung, strung, sung, hung, lung
–unk: punk, sunk, junk, hunk, dunk

Page 64
–unt: runt, hunt, blunt, grunt, stunt
–ush: gush, hush, lush, rush, brush

Page 65
–ust: dust, bust, gust, just, must
–ut: cut, gut, but, hut, nut

Page 66
–ar: star, jar, far, car, bar
–ard: hard, yard, guard, bard, card

Page 67
–ark: spark, bark, park, dark, shark
–art: cart, start, dart, part, chart

Page 68
–ew: dew, few, knew, new, pew
–oo: coo, boo, too, moo, zoo

Page 69
–ool: tool, school, pool, fool, cool
–oom: bloom, broom, room, doom, boom

Page 70
–oon: croon, spoon, soon, moon, noon
–oop: scoop, stoop, troop, loop, hoop

Page 71
–oot: scoot, shoot, root, hoot, boot
–ue: glue, true, blue, clue, due

Page 72
–all: ball, call, fall, hall, tall
–alk: talk, balk, walk, chalk, stalk

Page 73
–aw: gnaw, jaw, paw, saw, law
–awl: brawl, bawl, scrawl, drawl, crawl

Page 74
–awn: yawn, fawn, lawn, pawn, dawn
–ong: wrong, song, strong, throng, long

Page 75
–ore: core, bore, sore, wore, more
–ord: cord, ford, chord, sword, lord

Page 76
–orn: horn, corn, torn, born, worn
–ort: sort, port, short, fort, sport

Page 77
–oss: loss, toss, boss, cross, gloss
–oth: cloth, broth, moth, froth, sloth

Page 78
–ound: found, bound, hound, pound, round
–out: gout, pout, bout, out, rout

Page 79
–ow: cow, bow, how, now, vow
–own: gown, down, brown, clown, town

Page 80
–ask: task, cask, flask
–asp: gasp, clasp, grasp
–ax: tax, wax, lax

Page 81
–age: stage, cage, page
–aid: raid, maid, paid
–ait: strait, wait, bait

Page 82
–ase: case, base, vase
–aste: paste, taste, waste
–aint: saint, paint, faint

Page 83
–arm: farm, harm, charm
–arn: yarn, barn, darn
–arp: harp, sharp, tarp

Page 84
–ead: head, bread, dead
–ear: bear, wear, swear
–ealth: wealth, health, stealth

Page 85
–edge: ledge, wedge, hedge
–eft: theft, cleft, left
–eg: peg, leg, beg

Page 86
–elp: kelp, yelp, help
–em: them, stem, gem
–ense: tense, dense, sense

Page 87
–ep: step, pep, prep
–esh: flesh, fresh, mesh
–ex: flex, vex, hex

Page 88
–e: me, he, she
–ea: sea, pea, tea
–ead: bead, lead, read

Page 89
–eap: cheap, heap, leap
–ease: crease, lease, grease
–east: beast, least, feast

Page 90
–eech: screech, leech, speech
–ief: thief, brief, chief
–ield: yield, shield, field

Page 91
–ilk: milk, silk, bilk
–in: thin, chin, skin
–ish: fish, dish, wish

Page 92
–o: no, so, go
–oad: load, toad, road
–oal: goal, foal, coal

Page 93
–oast: coast, toast, roast
–oe: toe, Joe, hoe
–ost: most, post, ghost

Page 94
–ood: wood, good, stood
–ook: cook, book, look
–ould: would, could, should